NETWORK MARKETING QUEEN

NETWORK MARKETING QUEEN

*Your Guide to Creating Massive Success
by Owning Your Feminine Power*

DR. ERIN POLLINGER

LIONCREST
PUBLISHING

NETWORK MARKETING QUEEN
Your Guide to Creating Massive Success by Owning Your Feminine Power

ISBN   978-1-5445-0642-5 *Hardcover*
           978-1-5445-0640-1 *Paperback*
           978-1-5445-0641-8 *Ebook*

Author photo by Sarah Haywood.

I dedicate this book to mother, Ann Haas, who without, I would have no idea what being in my power truly looks like. Thank you, Mom, for fiercely loving me, for accepting me exactly as I am, for always showing up for me, and for supporting me in all the darkness and light that I have experienced in life. Your fire and passion for contribution has inspired me to bring forth my deepest gifts in service of helping others, and for that I am forever grateful. Your courage and willingness to be so unapologetically YOU, no matter what anyone thinks, has shaped me into who I am today. I love you infinitely.

I also dedicate this book to my father, Ken Pollinger. Thank you for showing me the way into the magical and mystical realms of life and for always encouraging me to question and seek a deeper level of truth. Thank you for your unconventional ways and beliefs and for sparking my curiosity of the esoteric. Thank you for guiding me to my path of chiropractic, yoga, meditation, and spirituality as this book would definitely not be in existence without these things in my life. Thank you for giving me the gifts of your profound wisdom and your hunger for always going deeper. I love you oceans and oceans and mountains and mountains.

Finally, I dedicate this book to my daughter, Willow Maya Keefe. Thank you for being the one who ultimately motivated and inspired me to be the best woman I could possibly be. From the moment you were born, I knew that I would keep growing and evolving until I was a woman that both you and I were proud of. Thank you for being so authentic and real, for always telling me exactly how you feel, for making me laugh and helping me not take any of this too seriously. Thank you for being my best friend for these past nineteen years. Thank you for your patience and support with all the traveling, phone calls, zooms and team building in these past two-and-a-half years, so that we can have a truly extraordinary life of infinite possibilities. You are and always will be the light of my life.

CONTENTS

INTRODUCTION

Simply holding this book in your hands means that you are on your way to creating a wildly successful business in network marketing with ease, energy, and joy. That much, I can promise.

Before you read further, I'd like you to sit somewhere that feels pleasurable and comfortable, put the book down, close your eyes, take a deep breath, and feel your body for a moment. Now, let the opening statement sink in: *You are meant to create a wildly successful business in network marketing with ease, energy, and joy.*

This book is like nothing you've read before, and my intention is that by the end you will feel drastically different about your life, your business, and yourself as a woman.

I get that this may seem impossible right now. I know how you feel, because I've been there.

You're feeling overwhelmed, exhausted, and disconnected from yourself, your business, your earning power, and those you love. You've been thinking about creating an incredible network marketing business, but you fear it's never going to get off the ground. You feel a lack of support, and it's often a struggle just to get through the day. You have huge dreams and aspirations, but no idea of how to get there. In fact, your dreams are starting to feel more and more fleeting and impossible to attain.

I want you to know that I am sorry.

I am so sorry it's been so hard for you. I am sorry that you are feeling alone and unsupported. I am sorry you have not been told every day that you are a beautiful, powerful, extraordinary woman with amazing gifts to share with the world. I am sorry that you were not told daily what a precious gift you are. I am sorry that you were not taught that you are an unlimited being in an unlimited universe in which anything you desire is possible. I am sorry that you have not known that you can be, do, and have whatever it is that your heart and soul deeply long for.

I am sorry you haven't been seen or heard.

I get it. I've been right there in your shoes. And I am here to assure you, that as women, we *can* have what we desire. We can create extraordinary lives that we are wild and crazy about, from a place of pleasure and power, while feeling fully fueled and alive. How do I know this? Because I am living it. And so can you.

FROM DISCONNECTED TO FULLY FUELED

Who am I anyway and why should you listen to me? Let me tell you a bit about myself and the path I have walked. When I was younger, I really struggled to discover my identity. I suffered from low self-esteem and wasn't quite sure where I fit in. When I was in high school, I used sex, alcohol, and drugs to help cope and find a sense of connection and belonging. Most of the time, I was unable to connect to my joy, energy, or light, and I did what I could to try to cover up my pain.

I graduated high school with straight A's—yes I was still an overachiever, which was another way I tried to avoid pain. In college, I continued using drugs and alcohol as a way to feel connected and part of something. I found myself in a very dark place as a result. I knew I needed to do something different or I would spiral down into a place that I wasn't willing to go. A chiropractic adjustment resulted in a life-altering experience of connecting to the peace, joy, and light inside of myself—and as a result I decided to enroll in chiropractic school. I graduated with honors when I was twenty-four years old. Shortly after, I became pregnant with my daughter and took over a very successful chiropractic practice in Berkeley, California.

I overworked and pushed myself as we were struggling financially. I was severely stressed out and wound up going into labor six weeks early. My daughter was born healthy, but my relationship with her father came apart under stress and ended three years later. The separation sent me into a tailspin of grief, despair, and deeper disconnection than I had ever felt before.

Although my ex was an incredible and present father, being a single mom was difficult to say the least. I was forced to be resourceful because I didn't have a partner to rely on for the day-in and day-out. I was the breadwinner, the cook, the cleaner, and the gardener. I was everything, and it took its toll.

I began suffering from severe physical symptoms that manifested as digestive and skin issues, which caused me to lose more of my self-confidence. I didn't want to get out of bed in the morning, much less leave the house. At times I wasn't sure how I would pay rent or put food on the table for my daughter. Those were dark days and I sometimes wondered if it would be way easier to run my car off the side of the road than to continue to live that way.

In my mid-thirties I reached a breaking point and found myself sobbing on my knees on the kitchen floor. It was then that I made a decision that my life was going to change. I decided that I was no longer going to be sick or broke.

Somewhere deep inside I knew that my gifts had to be shared, my voice had to be heard, and that my message was too big to live this way for even one more day. I made those decisions with every single bone in my body and didn't look back.

THE FEMININE CONNECTION

That breakdown, and breakthrough, was a long time in the making. I had spent years trying to find my power to varying levels of success. At one particularly low point, a friend introduced me to Tantric Dance of Feminine Power, which was an invitation to learn how to connect with my center—my womb—and to move from a new and different place in myself.

During the first class, I was extremely disconnected from this place that I now know is the key to moving from my feminine power. Once I began to connect with it, there was this immense uprising of grief, as I became aware of how alone, unsupported, and unheard I had felt for so long. I began to cry, and I actually cried every class for the first few months. After that initial phase of grief and *feeling* all of these emotions, I started moving into a deeper under-standing of what it truly means to be in my body and in my pleasure and power. This newfound power and boldness that I experienced motivated me to take my life back in all areas.

I became obsessed with learning all I could about how to make money. I took courses and paid for coaches using credit cards at first, because I didn't have the money. The better my relationship with money became, the more my health shifted, and my symptoms started to dissipate. I was so in awe of this health/wealth connection that I became a life coach focused on these two areas, while still working in my thriving chiropractic practice. I began supporting women to create lives they could be proud of in a way that felt alive and energized. I developed workshops and retreats in which I weaved in chiropractic and tantric dance with the intent of empowering women to move more from their pleasure and their power. It was around this time that my father and I opened our retreat center in Costa Rica, Tierra Sagrada de Costa Rica, where I have held retreats using these tools combined with the magic of nature to assist women in going deeper into this reconnection. By doing my own internal work, I found myself doing the things that truly brought me joy. It had all finally paid off and I was truly living a life that I absolutely loved.

FROM ORDINARY TO EXTRAORDINARY

When I turned forty, I decided I wanted to travel and have more freedom from my chiropractic practice. I wanted to inspire people, share my message on a bigger scale, and make money while I traveled, instead of being tied to an office. I wanted to be of a much higher-level service and have greater impact in the world. I wanted my life to be a ten in all areas: health, wealth, work, relationship, community, and spirituality. I was ready to move from ordinary to extraordinary! Also, my daughter was going to be leaving for college in a few years and it was time for me to reclaim ME in a whole new way. It was time. I had no idea *how* this was going to happen, but I knew enough at that point to know that the *how* was none of my business.

So I did what I teach all of the women I work with to do. Every morning in my meditation, I relaxed into my desire (without worrying about *how*), got into my pleasure and power, and made the nonnegotiable decision that I would have the life of my wildest dreams. I could see it, feel it, and was already living this life in my mind, heart, and soul. Shortly after doing this practice daily, I was introduced by two dear friends to the network marketing company I am now a part of. At first, I wondered if it was a cosmic joke because I knew this was the answer to my prayers, but I never in a million years thought it would involve network marketing! Needless to say, I said yes.

I won't lie; the beginning was hard. I already had a full plate with being a single mother, running a full-time chiropractic and life coach practice, doing workshops for women, and continuing to expand my retreat center in Costa Rica. I had no idea how I would fit one more thing into my already full schedule. However, I saw the big vision and made the decision to sleep less, be less social, and say no to things that weren't an absolute must. I reached out to friends, colleagues, and family at every break that I had. I did in-home presentations every single week, even if my dog was the only one who showed up to hear me speak.

I also struggled with the stigma of network marketing. I thought I was demoting myself from being a successful chiropractor and life coach, and I was actually quite embarrassed about now being part of this industry that can tend to have such a bad reputation. But, as I got to know it over the first few months, I learned that network marketing is truly about being of greater contribution and high-level service, while creating community and a legacy. It's about reclaiming financial freedom, taking your power back, and saying yes like you never have before. It's about thinking bigger and choosing to play a bigger game. It's about supporting others in a profound way and building extraordinary relationships. It's about taking your dreams and desires out from under the rug, dusting them off, and bringing them back to life.

In the short time that I've been part of this industry, I am now a true ambassador of what I believe is the most incredible profession out there. We get to turn people on to life-changing products while building teams within an incredible community of people. This journey of network marketing is beyond a shadow of a doubt one of the most incredible things I have ever done in my life.

THE NETWORK CONNECTION

As I grew into this new business endeavor, it was so much fun to see some major overlap between my work as a chiropractor and my work as a network marketer. In my chiropractic practice, I use methods of healing called Network Spinal Analysis (NSA) and Reorganizational Healing (ROH), both developed by Donald Epstein, D.C. When I recognized that the word "network" was in both network spinal analysis and network marketing—two journeys that had radically changed me and my life—I knew there was no mistake in the connection.

NSA is a revolutionary chiropractic technique that allows us, as chiropractors, to help our patients reorganize their nervous systems by making contacts along their spines to evoke waves that transform trauma into energy. These "spinal entrainments" help the body to be more aligned, connected, and energized. Through network chiropractic care, we reclaim parts of ourselves that have been disowned, denied, and rejected so that we can experience greater wholeness.

Being under NSA care since I was nineteen years old has helped me to become connected to my "internal community" and experience this wholeness. This then manifested on the outside as the ability to be more open to connect with my external community and build my network. Network chiropractic care and network marketing both serve to get you into full alignment, so that more energy is available to foster these internal and external connections and communities, which is crucial if you want to experience massive success in life. Both of these are journeys of profound personal growth.

Because of what has transpired in my life as a result of saying yes to this network marketing journey, I now focus primarily on my network marketing business as well as on my workshops and retreats supporting women to rise into feminine leadership. Within this space, I get to do what I absolutely love, every single day. For me, it's the only way. My goal is to show you the steps to live this way too.

FROM MAN-MODE TO FEMININE

Building my network marketing business was difficult in the beginning, because I pushed myself, overworked, and was close to being completely burned out. This was because I was operating in "man-mode." Even though I teach women how to create lives from a place of pleasure and power, I followed a model of business that wasn't sustainable. I found myself crying in the bathtub many evenings, and almost gave up several times.

In order to stay energized, and not burned out, I needed to do things in a drastically different way. I had to take a step back and realize that I wasn't putting into practice the methods that I teach others. I had to fully embrace the feminine principles I write about here. It was time to really walk my talk.

Once I did this, my business exploded in a way that felt absolutely amazing! I created a seven-figure business in just under two years, have over 30,000 people on my team,[1] and am the top female earner and third top earner overall. I now travel all over the world living a life of freedom and service. My life is a ten in ALL areas. I speak on stages to thousands of people, sharing my message and motivating and inspiring others to create lives they are madly and passionately in love with. I bring my gifts forth into the world in a way that has massive impact, which feels incredible. I am in my full power and pleasure and feel more radiant, magnetic, lit up, turned on, and energized than ever before.

This has been my experience, because I made a choice and I had the tools. After reading this book, you will have the power to make this choice too, and you will have the tools that you need to create a successful business from your feminine power. Massive success isn't meant for just a lucky few. It's meant for us all.

If I can do it, so can you.

---

[1] In network marketing we never make any guarantees or promises that you will make any money. This is my personal experience and may not be yours. You may make nothing in your network marketing business or you may make millions.

Note: I want you to know that by no means am I saying that I have mastered all that I write here in this book. I always teach that which I need to learn most. We, as women, are figuring out this together. I am simply sharing what has worked for me and I pray that it can work for you too.

SEASONS OF WELL-BEING

This isn't your typical network marketing success guide. While I will talk about connection with your downline, increasing sales, and building your network, you will not find here the normal tips you've heard elsewhere, or learned in your training. Instead, I will cover topics in a way that will support you to use your energy to get exactly what you desire and deserve.

One of these topics is the Seasons of Well-Being. This body of work, founded by Dr. Donald Epstein, is absolutely key to your success in your network marketing business. Just as we have seasons in nature, we have Seasons of Well-Being in our lives. Dr. Epstein writes in his book, *The 12 Stages of Healing: A Network Approach to Wholeness*, "When something is in season it's ripe, ready, and its time has arrived. For the human experience each season creates different opportunities, actions, and experiences."

The season you are in affects everything in your life including work, play, emotions, and decisions. The season supports and amplifies a particular way of being, thinking, feeling, acting, relating, and healing. The magic comes when we are aware of, acknowledge, and accept the season we are in and consciously call in more of the season where we need to be to live an extraordinary life.

In this book, I will show you how to move through these Seasons of Well-Being, as a woman, in a way that will support you to create massive success in your business from your pleasure and power. I will also help you to know that money can be easy and that you can have a fun and energized relationship with it. You will also learn, as I did, that you can be the Queen of your business and life.

You may wonder, "What does that even mean?" Everyone has their own idea of what being a Queen means. I'd like to talk for a minute about what the word means to me and how I refer to it throughout the book.

As a Queen, you know how to be with the parts of yourself that need listening to and give yourself the time to be fully with what is. You know how to take your power and passion back. You know what you truly desire and make the decision and commitment to only be available for whatever that is. You know how to say *no* and how to say *yes*. As a Queen, you are supported by a team, and you delegate often so that you get to do more of what you love and less of what you don't love.

As a Queen, you are able to drop into your pleasure and exist in a relaxed, energized state of being. You are in your body. You serve others at a high level. You feel grateful and connected. You know it's less about what you are *doing* and more about who you are *being*. You walk your talk. You pay attention to the way you dress and how you carry yourself. You own your beauty and feel at home in your body. You take exquisite care of yourself. You are fun, playful, and full of life force. You create your life as the feminine force of nature that you know yourself to be. You have a deep sense of who you are, why you are here, and you know your soul-aligned mission and purpose.

MY PRAYER FOR YOU

My prayer for you is that by reading this book, you will feel a sense of homecoming and connection to a part of yourself that truly changes you. I pray that you will come to see how creating massive success in your life can be fun. I pray that you will remember your most authentic, radiant, and powerful self, and start to own it on a cellular level. I pray that, through these pages you will find an infinite and endless well of support, energy, wisdom, and love within yourself. I pray that you will access the energy to fully step into the Queen that you are—of your business and your life.

I pray that you will connect more deeply with your inner community so that your outer community can unfold serendipitously. I pray that you will feel connected to all of the other women who read this book, knowing that we all have a story and that you are not alone. I pray that you will know I've got your back, and that everyone else reading this book has your back, too. You are part of this sisterhood.

I will never say that network marketing is always easy, fun, joyful, and pleasurable. It requires focus, commitment, and lots of action. There will absolutely be moments of despair and wanting to give up. You will cry, scream, and want to throw in the towel at times, but if you apply the principles presented in these pages, you will learn how to be with what is, harness greater levels of energy, and allow your business to build with a sense of effortlessness, grace, and magic.

Are you ready? Let's begin...

CHAPTER ONE

WOMBSPACE

Imagine having the ability to connect to a limitless source of support, energy, and wisdom that can fuel your life and your business. Now imagine that this source is within you and you can tap into it daily—or even multiple times a day. The bad news is most women have no idea this possibility even exists. The good news is that you have this ability available to you now and I will show you exactly how to access it.

NEWSFLASH: WOMEN ARE NOT MEN!

Women don't move like men. We don't talk like men. We don't walk like men. We don't think like men. And we certainly don't build businesses like men.

Unfortunately, women have been taught that in order to be successful, we need to be like men, bring out our masculinity, push aside emotions, and act in a cutthroat manner. We are taught that we need to take action and do more. We keep trying, but time and time again these methods fail and our businesses suffer for it. We find ourselves exhausted, burned out, and unable to achieve the success and freedom we desire.

MASCULINE IS NOT WRONG

Before we continue, I want to make something clear. Whether we are women or men, we *all* have both feminine and masculine parts. I am in no way making the masculine "wrong" and the feminine "right" in this book. I believe that both women and men are overworked, under-fueled, and could use a good dose of feminine power. Culture and society have—for the most part—taught us that to be successful we must use more of our masculine parts, while disowning the feminine ones. In following the principles in this book and reclaiming our feminine power, we become more whole—and I believe from there, anything is possible. Although this book is written for women and the practices are also meant for women, men can find the overall concepts valuable as well.

So how do we move more from our feminine power in business? Let me introduce you to a concept called *wombspace*. My relationship and connection with this place within myself have changed everything for me when it comes to building my business, and it can for you too.

HOMECOMING

Your wombspace is the physical and energetic space where your actual womb is. I call it wombspace because many women have had their wombs removed for various reasons, however the magic of wombspace lives in all women. In connecting to your wombspace, you will find a portal to your true desires and the divine, and an infinite amount of pleasure and power. When you are connected to your wombspace you are connected to your inner Queen. Imagine it as a temple or sacred space within that you can come home to every day and tap into the infinite resource of energy, support, and wisdom always available to you.

It takes a tremendous amount of energy for us to create lives that we feel over the moon wild and crazy about. We are supporting teams, making calls, presenting, having endless meetings, and traveling to build our global businesses, all while we are mothers, partners, wives, daughters, and all the things we are to so many people. We often forget about ourselves in order to give in service to others. Eventually this will take its toll. We must be able to come home, over and over again, to a place from which we can refuel.

Wombspace is that place.

THE WOMB IS THE PORTAL TO THE DIVINE

The divine is the inspired voice that serves to guide you—
you may call it God, Goddess, the Universe, source, spirit,
nature, or one of dozens of other names. It is your partner
and ally in creating what you desire. For me, going into
nature is the primary way I connect with the divine.

As I learned more about the womb, I came to realize just
how many ways it is connected to nature and the divine.

*"Menstruation is linked to nature via the cycles of the earth,
the moon, and the sun. For example, there are thirteen
moon cycles in a calendar year, and the average age a
girl first menstruates is thirteen years old. Both the moon's
cycle and the average woman's menstrual cycle last 29.5
days. The average woman's menstrual cycle lasts four
weeks and there are four seasons in a year. The average
age of menopause is fifty-two, which is also the number
of weeks in a year."*

—KARA MARIA ANANDA

When we connect to our womb, we connect with something so much bigger than ourselves. I believe, and have
come to know, that wombspace holds infinite wisdom that
we can all access.

SLOWING DOWN TO SPEED UP

We, as women, move way too fast. Most of us do everything
ourselves and we don't have the support that we need to get
out of the rat race and slow down. When we run in circles,
trying to check off the never-ending to-do list, we are not
available to receive the success that we desire. Homecoming to wombspace provides the opportunity repeatedly to

slow down, to breathe, and to reconnect to our desires, our pleasure, and our power. Only when we slow down can we access the energy needed to build massively successful businesses in a way that feels sustainable, without creating burnout or constant overwhelm.

As I mentioned earlier, in the beginning of my network marketing journey, I was in constant action and was moving in man-mode. I felt exhausted, overwhelmed, and completely unhappy, even though I was experiencing success in my growing business. It wasn't until I began slowing down and connecting to wombspace daily that I felt energized, connected, and in my full joy—*and* my business skyrocketed in a short period of time to where I truly desired it to be. Without doing the practices in this book and having an alive relationship with this part of myself, I would have given up a long time ago.

GETTING OUT OF SURVIVAL MODE

One of the gifts of connecting to your wombspace is the ability to access your true desires.

Most women have no idea what they really want, because we—as potentially limitless creatures—often exist in a state of fight or flight. As a chiropractor of twenty years, my job has been to assess this level of fight or flight in all the patients I see. And I can tell you—after evaluating posture, tension, and all of the other indicators of sympathetic overload—that most women are in severe survival mode.

When you suffer from trauma—physical, emotional, and/or chemical—and don't have the tools to deal with it, you get stuck in this way of being. Your primitive brain then does the thinking and you move from your unconscious brain rather than your conscious brain. You react from your head, not your heart (and certainly not from your wombspace). You feel exhausted, overwhelmed, lonely, and worried. You can't get in touch with your true desires because it's hard enough just to make it through the day having completed the necessary tasks to be a boss, wife, mother, daughter, and friend.

Sound familiar?

When you are in fight or flight, connecting with your wombspace is nearly impossible. As a woman, it is very important to do the things that support you to move from this state of sympathetic overload into a parasympathetic state. It is only then that you can slow down, relax, and begin to connect to this new and foreign place of wombspace. The two most potent ways I have found to get out of fight or flight, and back into alignment, is through chiropractic and taking hemp extract which is, in my opinion, the most important and powerful supplement on the planet.

Getting into alignment is critical because this is when the

frontal lobe of the brain wakes up. This is the part of the brain that allows you to make healthy, conscious choices and decisions that will help you get from where you are to where you desire to be. It is also at this point that we can connect to wombspace.

THE WOMBSPACE CONNECTION

Why is connection to wombspace such a game changer? Let's think about it. The womb is the source of creation. It is the place where the sperm and egg implant to create new life. It is where the fetus is held and nourished as it grows. When you connect to this place you have greater access to the energy of creation and can use it as fuel for your business.

A true Queen knows what she wants. Your connection with wombspace allows you to harness the energy of creation, access your deepest desires, remember the life you want to create for yourself, and tap into the resources that will bring this into reality.

You will also find that your desires, when connected to wombspace, are authentic and real. This authenticity allows you to *trust* your desires and know that they are the key to you living a life of freedom and success. Our desires are holy and are the seeds from which our life blossoms. Our first job as women is to know what our true desires are and to relax into them without worrying about the *how*. Then we fuel these desires with pleasure.

THE POWER OF PLEASURE

Most women are deeply disconnected from their pleasure. Developing a relationship with your wombspace can help reestablish this connection as it is an endless resource of pleasure—both sexually and non-sexually. When you have an orgasm of your uterus (which is absolutely possible) it is the deepest type of orgasm and comes with incredible pleasure.

Non-sexually, the more you connect with your wombspace, the more you can access the pleasure that arises from the relaxation, energy, grounding, and the ability to pause and be present in the moment. You are able to move out of your head and into your body when you have a relationship with your wombspace, which is truly a game changer. Embodiment is key to creating massive success by owning your feminine power!

Pleasure also comes from being connected to the divine. When we feel held by this bigger thing, we know we are not alone. We can relax and open. Additionally, connecting to our desire through cultivating a relationship with our wombspace brings tremendous pleasure. When we know what we want, we are able to expand beyond our current "groundhog day" reality, which is exciting and full of potential.

THE CONNECTION BETWEEN PLEASURE AND DESIRE

The *Feminine Operating System*, a term coined by Christina Morassi, an extraordinary coach I have worked with for years, shows us the connection between pleasure and desire. Desire is the first seed of creation where everything begins. In network marketing, and any business, it is critical that we have a *lot* of desires. We desire freedom, travel, and to be of greater contribution and service. We desire to live luxuriously and give back generously. We desire to earn a specific amount of money. We desire to achieve a specific rank. We desire to enroll a specific number of affiliates. We desire to build incredible teams and communities. These desires fuel our mission and purpose.

Again, most women are disconnected from what they truly want. It is an art to know your true desires. What you *think* you desire is probably different from what you *really* desire. Following the practices in this book and developing a relationship with your wombspace will help you access these deeper, more authentic desires.

After relaxing into your desires, without worrying about the *how*, it's time to get into your pleasure. Why? Because, the pleasure fuels the desire! Pleasure is like the water, sun, and nourishment that helps the seeds of desire grow. You can find pleasure in connecting with your wombspace, laying out in the sun, or doing yoga. You find pleasure in hanging out with your girlfriends or taking a relaxing stroll along the beach. You can find pleasure in dancing or eating your favorite foods. There are an infinite number of ways to get into your pleasure.

This process of using pleasure to fuel desire is opposite of the way most women operate. It is common for women to start with the desire and then go into action. They think, "I want to make $10,000 a month." Then, they want to know how. "How can I make this money?" Well, let me tell you ladies—the *how* is none of your business. Moving from the *how* is man-mode. For a woman to build her business in a way that feels energized and fun, she must start with desire and then get into her pleasure to fuel that desire. This is a revolutionary concept that we will talk about more (and experience) in the following pages.

THE WOMBSET-MINDSET CONNECTION

I used to believe success was 80 percent mindset and 20 percent structure, but as I learned more about the neuroscience of pleasure, I discovered that getting into our pleasure changes our mindset. How does this work? Pleasurable acts release nitric oxide, which causes your brain to be more neuroplastic, allowing for new thoughts which lead to new actions. In essence, pleasure can help reroute your brain pathways and change your mindset!

Pleasure also increases neuropeptides like opioids, endorphins, dopamine (also known as the "creativity wonder drug"), and oxytocin (which is produced as a result of a close, loving connection with another or self)—resulting in a "pleasure cocktail" that further reroutes the pathways to your brain.[2]

Enter self-love. When you are connected to your wombspace, you have a deeper appreciation and love for your precious and unique feminine essence. You feel more sensual, alive, and proud to be a woman. It may take time to get to this place, but in doing the practices daily, you will undoubtedly have this experience. So, even if you are not in a partnership, connecting with wombspace and practicing self-love raises the oxytocin levels.

When you combine pleasure and self-love, the pleasure cocktail is in full force and your brain is rewired for you to be in your power. You are more confident, goal-oriented, motivated, assertive, and talkative. You care less what others think, and you are more able to make decisions and commitments that are critical for building your business. I always tell my team that making the decision to succeed

2   This is a term coined by Eva Clay, MSW, LCSW, CHT

at a high level is a necessary requirement to win. You make that decision by getting into your power as a result of being in your pleasure. Again, this is all backed by science!

Pleasure also opens your receiving channels so that you can *receive* your desires. For the most part, most women have difficulty receiving, which prevents them from experiencing the success they desire in their business. Christina Morassi always says, "Having is the wanting, pleasure is the receiving!" And how do we connect with our pleasure? Through connecting to wombspace.

With all of this in mind, I came to realize that for women, in business and nearly everything in life, success is achieved 40 percent through what I call "wombset," 40 percent through mindset, and 20 percent through structure. Wombset affects mindset, and as we all know, your thoughts create your reality. This is why it is imperative to cultivate this relationship with wombspace, which will help your mind get into alignment with what you desire.

When you are connected to this magnificent resource, you are connected to your desire, your pleasure, and your feminine power. This ultimately supercharges you with energy, makes you radiant and attractive, and allows you to build your business with a greater level of serendipity and grace.

And who doesn't want that?

In the next three chapters, we will explore moving through the Seasons of Well-Being with your wombspace, laying out a roadmap for you to create massive success in your business and life. You will learn what it means to be the willing woman, the wise woman, and the wild woman—being fully with what is, embracing your pleasure, and owning your power so that you can create all that you desire.

EXERCISE: CONNECTING WITH YOUR WOMBSPACE

It's time to dive in and connect with your wombspace. This exercise serves as a starting point for cultivating this relationship that will change you *and* your life.

Find a quiet place where you are free from distractions and disruptions. If possible, find a place where you feel relaxed and are able to soften into a new part of yourself.

Sit in an upright position, either in a chair with your spine aligned or straddling a few pillows on the floor with your feet tucked behind you. Don't recline or slouch. Have an accentuated lumbar curve. Your pelvis must have the ability to move. Close your eyes and place your hands, palm over palm, about two inches below the navel, which is where your wombspace is located.

Say hello. Acknowledge your amazement that *this* is the place. Be curious. Most women are disconnected from their wombspace, so saying hello brings awareness and attention to the area.

Open your jaw slightly so that it is loose. Relax your shoulders and your face. Let all of your excess mental energy move down into your pelvis, almost like liquid honey dripping down your spine to gather in your pelvic bowl.

Tune into your breath and begin to breathe into your belly and your wombspace. Most women breathe only into their chest, which causes neck and shoulder tension. When you inhale into wombspace your belly will expand and your pelvis will rock forward. As you exhale, your belly comes back toward the spine and your pelvis will rock back.

Breathe and be aware. Be aware of the now and allow whatever is to be. If you feel disconnected, that's okay. If you feel areas of pain, that's okay. Just breathe and gently rock your pelvis as your belly expands and retracts. Feel yourself developing a connection with your wombspace through the breath and movement and just be with whatever is present. With each breath, allow yourself to feel more connected, relaxed, and energized.

Now, imagine your wombspace as your temple.

This place is a magical, mystical place that belongs only to you. See it as an actual physical space or room. You get to decorate it however you desire. Maybe it has sheepskin rugs with candles and red velvet pillows, an alter, or a magnificent view framed by white flowing curtains. Adorn your temple and make it a space in which you feel held and are able to drop into a relaxed and open state of being. Whenever you do your wombspace meditation, you will go to this temple and find it a resource of peace, support, energy, and homecoming. You can go to your temple daily or multiple times a day as needed. If you're feeling overwhelmed, stressed, or in need of support—you can access that support right here.

Do this exercise for five minutes and acknowledge any feelings that arise. There is no goal or outcome. You are simply feeling what is and remaining curious. End the five minutes with gratitude—giving thanks for this newfound connection and this new relationship with your wombspace.

Your journey has started. By anchoring into this exercise and connecting with your wombspace, you have begun to cultivate a relationship that will change who you are and how you move in the world.

 To receive the bonus audio meditation that accompanies this chapter, visit: networkmarketingqueen.com.

JOURNAL: YOUR TEMPLE

Where is your temple? How is it adorned? How do you feel in your temple? Describe what your temple looks like in the space below.

....

....

....

....

....

....

....

....

....

What did you notice as you connected to wombspace? (pain, disconnection, relaxation, curiosity, irritation, sadness, energy, joy?)

CHAPTER TWO

FEELING: THE WILLING WOMAN

"For a seed to achieve its greatest expression, it must come completely undone. The shell cracks, its insides come out and everything changes. To someone who doesn't understand growth, it would look like complete destruction."

—CYNTHIA OCCELLI

Have you ever felt completely disconnected, alone, and unsupported by life?

Have you ever felt endlessly triggered, blaming yourself and others for the circumstances of your life?

Have you ever felt frustrated because you are still stuck...in your body, around money, or in life in general?

You fear this situation is never going to end. You can't do it anymore. You want to give up. You are exhausted. You blame others, blame yourself, judge others, and judge yourself. You're triggered endlessly by relationships. You're on the gerbil wheel, trying so hard to get somewhere and make a breakthrough, but it's just not happening.

This is the Season of Discover.

You may experience these feelings in your personal life, your business, or both. The network marketing journey is one of such profound personal growth because it brings forth our darkest sides and deepest shadows. These parts surface as your team grows. The bigger you expand in your business, the more opportunity you have to really look at these places within. You want to experience massive success in network marketing. It's why you picked up this book! But, you might feel alone and isolated. You may feel unsupported by those above and below you on your team. You may fear you don't have what it takes. You may even fear you don't deserve success and that it is just not a possibility for you.

WOUNDING OF THE FEMININE

Women have been so badly wounded through culture, society, and the patriarchy. Media and advertising make us think we need to be a size two, have perfectly clear skin, and wear the best brands in order to feel loved and feel beautiful. We are constantly comparing ourselves to others and never feel that we are enough.

In the Season of Discover, when we connect to wombspace, we connect to all of the feminine wounding that resides here. There is much pain that lives in this place—sexual abuse, miscarriages, infertility, traumatic birthing experiences, and all of the ways we have been shamed or haven't felt seen, heard, loved, or supported.

Connecting to wombspace can bring these emotions and experiences to the surface. As I mentioned before, I cried in my tantric dance class for the first several months I attended. In the beginning I couldn't even move from that part of my body. I was a gymnast for the first thirteen years of my life, and considered myself to be quite embodied, but the reality was that I was so disconnected from this place that, when I tried to move from it, I felt paralyzed. Once I connected to my wombspace, I was able to access the deep well of grief, loss, and despair that resided here.

The Season of Discover allows us to become aware of our wombspace and the ways in which our precious feminine essence has been hurt, neglected, denied, or alienated. We discover that we have done so much in our lives to avoid this pain because it is much easier to not feel it at all. In this season, we become aware of how alone, exhausted, unheard, unseen, defeated, hopeless, and stuck we feel.

Most women are just trying to get through the day. We don't have the time or energy to get into our desire, because we are disconnected and in survival mode. We want to be connected to our desire—our desire to live amazing lives, travel to beautiful places, and indulge in relaxing spa days. Our desire to be loved and supported by partners who show up powerfully for us, because we are tired and burned out. Our desire to have the freedom to do what we love and spend more time with the people we care about. Our desire to give our soul gifts more fully. We have worked our asses off to try and get there, but still feel alone, unsupported, and stuck. We are worried and fear that we are not going to succeed in our businesses. (I say "we" in these statements because I still feel this way at times!)

You see, the goal isn't to graduate from feeling this way. The goal is to have the tools to be *with* these feelings when they come up in a different way, allowing us to really feel them.

This moves us into the triple A's.

THE TRIPLE A'S

Awareness, acknowledgment, and acceptance. These are the triple A's and the keys to receiving the gifts of the Season of Discover—and all of the seasons for that matter.[3]

---

3   This is also part of the Seasons of Well-Being work created by Dr. Donald Epstein.

The first step is becoming **aware** that you've been avoiding your feelings and emotions around the ways your feminine essence has been wounded. You have to be willing to connect with your wombspace and *feel* all of the pain that is present, becoming aware of the pain, struggle, suffering, grief, and disconnection. We then must **acknowledge** it without trying to change it. Lastly, we must **accept** what is. Know that it is normal and okay to feel this way. These feelings are a part of you. Don't push them away or try to get rid of them. Rather, say something as simple as, "Hi. I see you. I hear that you are stressed and would rather fall off a bridge than carry on. It's okay. You have a place within me and I accept you."

In order to create massive success, this acceptance piece is key. You might ask, "How can I, or why should I, accept something that feels negative or challenging?" Here's why. Every single challenging life circumstance or emotion is divinely orchestrated to shape you into who it is that you are meant to become. The deeper the wound, the greater the gift. If you can value these things and fully accept them, even if they have caused you tremendous suffering, there is a greater level of energy instantly available to allow those things to change (even though that is not the goal).

Most women have been taught to be strong and ignore their emotions, especially the ones viewed as negative. We avoid being with these parts like the plague. We don't want to sit in the space of awareness and acknowledgment and face our biggest fears. Instead we distract ourselves by over-working, losing ourselves in social media, or drowning in alcohol or drugs. What we resist persists, and when we push the parts that we don't want to feel under the rug and avoid them, they unconsciously sabotage our businesses and lives. Unfortunately, we can't win at network market-ing—or life—without facing our shadows and being willing to go into the darkness.

When we are able to become aware of, acknowledge, and accept all of our dark parts—as well as our light parts—the result is a stronger and more whole internal community. As I said before, this is where success in network market-ing begins. It is only when we have these thriving *internal* connections and communities that we can create *external* connections and communities. The more willing we are able to deeply feel these parts and accept them as part of us, the more available we are for success.

It takes bravery and a willingness to be still so that you can become aware of, acknowledge, and accept what is. Only when we can connect with these darker parts can we begin to heal. It is when we avoid and deny these parts that they unconsciously sabotage our business and lives. In network marketing, it's imperative that we are willing to be with these parts in the Season of Discover daily, because this business will make you want to shout, cry, and scream. This business can, and will at times, drag you down, and if you don't have the tools to deal with the darker parts that come up, I promise you, you will quit.

I don't want you to quit. I want you to succeed. The key to having more energy and moving forward is sitting with *what is* in Season of Discover.

Each week I conduct a coaching call for my team. At the beginning of the call, we dive into the Season of Discover together. We get to become aware of, acknowledge, and accept the parts that are feeling challenged, scared, triggered alone, and unworthy. There is so much power in doing this in community and I believe these calls are critical for my team as they now have a place each week to be with what is so that they can then have increased energy to move forward.

And succeeding in life is all about energy! When we move through life avoiding what's true in any given moment, we experience a very low level of energy. The result is that we minimize. We minimize money, relationships, and opportunities because we don't have the energy to manage them. When we practice the triple A's in the Season of Discover, there is more energy available to create lives filled with massive success and freedom.

GETTING TRIGGERED

Being massively successful in network marketing requires

that you support and hold a huge team. This industry is all about relationships, which unfortunately comes with many opportunities to be triggered by others—or do some triggering of your own.

When we have not become aware of, acknowledged, and accepted all of our different parts, the beautiful parts *and* the ugly parts—guess what happens? We get triggered. Whenever we judge or blame someone else for something, it is ultimately because we have not become aware of, acknowledged, and accepted those parts within ourselves. And we women can be so good at playing the blame game, especially when it comes to blaming ourselves. It's been shown that women are more likely than men to attack themselves and go into self-doubt and self-blame when they fail or do something "wrong."

This is just one of the many reasons why network marketing is such an incredible journey of personal development, growth, and evolution. When we are willing to become aware of the ways that we judge and blame others as well as ourselves, along with having acceptance all of our different parts, we get less triggered. We are then more capable of supporting others when they get triggered too, which helps them feel more cared for, loved, and seen.

The next time you find yourself triggered by someone on your team, I support you to pause and look at where these pieces that you are blaming or judging live inside of you. Can you stop and become aware of, acknowledge, and accept them? This will create more love, acceptance, and connection within your team, which will ultimately magnetize more people to it. Nobody wants to be on a team in which there is unspoken hurt or issues that are unresolved. Again, it's all energy, and people will feel this and be less attracted.

It is not until the end of Season of Discover that we begin to take responsibility for our lives. We now have the energy to forgive those who have wounded us and can access the ability to truly apologize to the parts of ourselves that have felt unworthy, undeserving, incapable, alone, unsupported, unheard, and unseen. We fully accept how frustrated we have been, having tried so hard to make a breakthrough with no success, and remember that we are not a victim. We know that our lives are as they are because of the choices we have made, and that we can now make new ones. We are now able to get in touch with our authentic desires and move more powerfully into what it is that we are choosing to create.

In the next chapter we will be talking about the Season of Awaken and the Wise Woman. Before we can harness our power, we need to get connected, fueled and super energized by getting more into our pleasure. Remember, as women, we first need to be willing to be with what is. Then, we have more energy to connect with our desires. After that, we fuel the desires with pleasure. Finally, we are able to take our power back and go out and take action. So now, let's dive into connection, pleasure, and flow, so that we can then own our feminine power and create massive success!

EXERCISE: BEING WITH WHAT IS

Sit in your wombspace connecting position. Close your eyes and place your hands, palm over palm, on your wombspace.

Relax and start to breathe. As you breathe in, your belly gets bigger and your pelvis rocks forward. As you breathe out, your belly moves back towards your spine and your tailbone moves between your legs.

Go into your temple, where you feel held, supported and resourced with energy. Say hello to your wombspace.

Start to notice and become aware of the parts within you that are in the Season of Discover. These parts may feel alone, unsupported, overwhelmed, disconnected, unworthy, scared, or hopeless. You may feel like it's never going to end and that it would be easier to just give up. Perhaps you find yourself blaming or judging others or yourself. Maybe you are getting endlessly triggered. Perhaps you feel stuck and frustrated because you've been working so hard with no results.

Stay connected to wombspace, breathe, and just be present with this awareness. Acknowledge these parts by saying out loud, "Sometimes it feels like it's never going to end. Sometimes I feel so alone. Sometimes it feels like I just want to give up. Sometimes I feel so disconnected. Sometimes I feel completely hopeless." If you feel emotion, express it. If you don't feel emotion, you may want to make a sound as you exhale. This will begin to express any emotions that are there but are not ready to be fully expressed. If you are frustrated because you are still not where you want to be, you may want to make a loud sound and say "I am so stuck!" The most important thing is to acknowledge these parts of you without trying to change them. Stay here for several minutes.

Acknowledge and accept that there are parts of yourself that you love and parts you don't love. There are wild parts and contained parts. There are beautiful parts and ugly parts. There are motivated parts and lazy parts. There are parts that are so scared and parts that trust so deeply. You have all of these different parts, and the Season of Discover is where you recognize that you are a dynamic human with a variety of feelings and emotions.

The next step is to create a Healing Guide. Women often feel very alone. We need allies, especially from within. Having a strong internal team allows us to build a strong external team. Having been a single mother for almost thirteen years, I have received endless and invaluable support from my internal team of guides.

It is now time for you to create your own Healing Guide. This being is someone who is benevolent, powerful, loving, and 100 percent has your back. She can be a goddess, power animal, teacher, or mentor. Bring your Healing Guide into your temple. Feel her support and love and let her know that you are excited to cultivate a relationship with her.

Now, get in touch with your *little girl*. This is the part of you that carries all of your wounds. Bring into your awareness this little one who has been so badly hurt. She wasn't seen, she wasn't heard, and she wasn't loved the way she wanted to be. Take a few moments just to be with her. Now, apologize to her. Say, "I'm so sorry that you have felt so alone. I'm so sorry you weren't heard, I'm so sorry you weren't seen. I'm so sorry that it's been so hard for you. I'm so sorry that you weren't told that you are a precious gift every single day. I'm so sorry that you have felt so stuck." Assure her that it hasn't yet been time for the breakthrough and that her life is unfolding in divine timing.

Let her know you see her now, you are here for her, and she is okay exactly as she is. Usher her into the arms of your

Healing Guide. Ask your Healing Guide if she is willing to do a healing with this part of yourself. Notice what happens. Be present with this for as long as you need. This may bring up emotion. Allow your Healing Guide to support you in deeply feeling these emotions. Thank your Healing Guide for continuing to heal this part of yourself in your subconsciousness for the upcoming hours, days, weeks, and months.

Let these images fade and return to your connection with wombspace. Continue the breath and movement here for another two or three minutes, allowing whatever is present to just be.

The beauty of this practice is that when you are in Season of Discover and feel challenged, you can connect to wombspace and go into your temple to find strength and support.

 To receive the bonus audio meditation that accompanies this chapter, visit: networkmarketingqueen.com.

Document what you felt, saw, or discovered in your meditation for Season of Discover. Get specific in the feelings and emotions you became aware of—suffering, disconnection, hopelessness, frustration, triggers, or being stuck in your current reality. Acknowledge those feelings and fully accept them as part of you. Remember, when we try to push these parts away and get rid of them, they only get stronger and sabotage our lives.

....

....

....

....

....

....

....

....

....

JOURNAL: HEALING GUIDE

Describe your Healing Guide. What does she look like? What is she wearing? What is her presence like? How does she move? What qualities does she embody?

....

....

....

....

....

....

....

....

....

....

CHAPTER THREE

BEING: THE WISE WOMAN

"No one and nothing outside of you can give you salvation, or free you from the misery. You have to light your own lamp. You have to know the miniature universe that you yourself are."
—BANANI RAY, AWAKENING INNER GURU

Have you ever been so in the flow of your life that things just unfold with a sense of ease and grace?

Have you ever felt like your life and business are unfolding like magic?

Have you ever felt as if the Universe is putting the perfect people that you are meant to connect with right in front of you?

You feel supported and full of energy. You feel grateful...just because. You are grateful for all the gifts you've been given, and you give your gifts fully in service to others. You are more focused on *who you are being* than *what you are doing*. You deeply trust the unfolding of life and feel connected to something much bigger than yourself. You know how to get into your pleasure and your receiving channels are wide open. You are magnetic and attractive, and your business is unfolding like magic, with an incredible level of serendipity and grace. You feel resourced and part of a larger community, within which you give your gifts and receive the gifts of others.

This is the Season of Awaken.

In the Season of Awaken, your desires are greater and more extraordinary. You think and dream bigger as you come to know yourself as a limitless being. You have a profound level of love and appreciation for yourself. You are a beacon of light, an agent of change, and a global visionary leader. You are relaxed and derive an enormous amount of pleasure from both your deep trust of the timing of your life's unfolding as well as your connection with the giving and receiving of the limitless energy that is you.

You are joyful and in the flow. Gratitude and awe are two of the primary emotions you feel throughout the day. You are building a massively successful network marketing business in a way that is exciting and fun, and has you bounding out of bed each morning.

Can I get a hell yes?!

DEVELOPING YOUR SOUL-ALIGNED MISSION AND PURPOSE

In the Season of Awaken you are in alignment with your soul's mission and purpose. In network marketing this is sometimes referred to as your *why*. In my experience, over time your *why* transforms into your deeper mission and purpose.

When I first began my network marketing journey, my *why* was very different than it is today. Part of my *why* was a desire for greater freedom to travel, while giving my gifts and making money. Another part of my *why* was to earn the money to send my daughter, Willow, to college. As a single mother at the time, giving her this gift was extremely important to me, and I literally had no money saved when I began my network marketing journey. I also wanted to earn more money to continue building out my retreat center in Costa Rica with my father, as we had run out of money to do so. I am so proud to say that I have accomplished both of those things in the short two and a half years that I have been involved with my company.

My *why* then became my deeper mission and purpose.

Your soul-aligned mission and purpose stems from your core desires. These core desires are the things most important to you. There is no *wrong* desire, as you will only have those desires that are meant for you. Desires are holy and guide you to your next step.

My personal core desires are energy, service, community, freedom, limitlessness, luxury, generosity, health, and wealth.

From there, I developed my soul-aligned mission and purpose: *To help people remember that they are unlimited beings in an unlimited universe; while reclaiming their most energized relationships with their bodies, money, and life itself. I create a community within which we attract millions, inspire millions, live luxuriously, and give back generously.*

And while that is still true for me, my mission has expanded to support women to know that they can build a massively successful business from their pleasure and feminine power, in a way that feels energized and fun. This mission and purpose are what led me to write this book!

In network marketing, or any business, you *must* know your soul-aligned mission and purpose, because that is what drives your business. People are subconsciously more attracted to your mission and purpose than they are to your product or business opportunity.

Again, your *why* can change. It *will* change, especially as you navigate through the Seasons of Well-Being. In the Season of Discover, your *why* may be, "I need to pay my rent and put food on the table for my child." As I mentioned, the Season of Discover is a low energy season and thus a low energy desire. In the Season of Awaken, your *why* transforms into your mission and purpose statement. It may be, "My mission is to create a global foundation to build schools around the world and help one million children receive education."

Connecting to your wombspace will help you more authentically know your desires, which will lead to your *why*, and then that will change to be your soul-aligned mission and purpose. All you need to do is slow down, connect, ask, and listen.

ATTRACTIVE, MAGNETIC, AND RECEPTIVE

Your customers and downline will be attracted to your particular soul-aligned mission and purpose and the community you are creating. They may come for the product and the business initially, but they stay for the community. Network marketing requires strong team cultures and communities, and it is important to look at how you bring people together to experience this.

I am personally committed to attracting women (and men of course, but we are focusing on women here) who are open to receiving the support that I offer. Not everyone is open to my beliefs, but the women who join my team and plug into the weekly zoom meetings I hold for them really start to feel the magic. I help them remember that network marketing can be something that feeds them in a profound way and that building a business can be fun and energized. These women feel part of the circle of sisterhood that I have created.

Often times in network marketing, and in business in general, women are competitive, gossipy, and don't truly have each other's backs. We get jealous and compare ourselves to one another. We have forgotten what true sisterhood means. These weekly meetings are a place where women come to be celebrated and seen, and a time where they receive a huge resource of support and energy.

At a recent conference, over one hundred women from my team met before the opening event. I took them on a journey of the Seasons of Well-Being with their wombspace, similar to what I am sharing in this book. It was a truly extraordinary experience. They laughed, danced, cried, and got into their power and pleasure in a whole new way. They left the meeting feeling fueled, energized, and open to receiving all of the wisdom, training, and connections that the next three days would offer. They also felt more magnetic and trusting that their business would build with greater ease and serendipity.

In the Season of Awaken, you are attractive, magnetic, and receptive because you are in alignment and fueled with pleasure—and you attract people that are like you, who share your big vision and, to some extent, your same soul-aligned mission and purpose. This is where the magic unfolds.

STAYING FUELED WITH PLEASURE

To stay fueled with the energy in the Season of Awaken we must remain connected with our pleasure. As I mentioned before, women are so often disconnected from their pleasure because of conditioning from society, religion, and culture that tells us it is shameful and wrong to feel good and be in your bliss. This could not be further from the truth. When a woman is in her pleasure, she is lit up, radiant, and full of passion and energy to shine her light and give her gifts in service. She blesses and inspires all that she touches.

RECLAIMING YOUR PLEASURE

If you find yourself getting triggered by the word *pleasure* or by this idea of staying fueled with pleasure, chances are there is a part of you that has been wounded. Perhaps you need to acknowledge any feelings of shame or fear—or tend further to your little girl who has been taught to play small and not own her right to be a fully embodied woman in her pleasure. This is an incredible opportunity for you to go deeper into reclaiming your wholeness.

One of the best ways to stay fueled with pleasure is to take at least one full day per week off to unplug and focus on you. Put work aside and be present with the people you love, sit in stillness, walk in nature, and do the things that make you feel alive and juicy. On the days you work, take pleasure breaks to refuel. Several times a day, stop for five to ten minutes to take a quick nap, lay in the sun, or have a short dance party with yourself. And remember to connect with wombspace, which is your infinite resource of pleasure.

RETURN TO THE MAGIC

As children, we lived in a place of magic and fairy tales. Anything was possible. We were kings and queens and our imaginations were limitless. Society then taught us that we are not magical and that we have limits. We were taught various rules and were then told we can only be successful if we follow those rules. In the Season of Discover, we are still victims to the rules and beliefs that we carry. In the Season of Awaken, we remember that we are magical and return to that place of infinite possibility. We return to the land of play and freedom where we experience our biggest, most beautiful dreams.

MERMAID MEDITATION

I love to keep it playful in my business. One of the ways I love supporting my women is by guiding them through my mermaid meditation.

In network marketing we refer to huge players as "whales." Whales are successful, determined, community-oriented, connected, and badasses with heart. They are fun to work with, they are very independent, and they don't need constant hand-holding. They see the big vision, have soul-aligned missions, and are instrumental in the massive explosion of your business.

The meditation goes like this:

Connect with your wombspace and begin activating this space with breath and movement of your pelvis. Let yourself melt and relax more deeply with every breath. Feel your spine as liquid, allowing the waves of movement to ripple through it. Let this energize you and bring you into your pleasure.

Now, imagine you are a mermaid swimming in the crystal clear, blue-green waters of the ocean. The sunlight pierces the water, making it sparkle like diamonds. You are attractive and magnetic, and you are fueled by connection with everything. You are a brilliant, blinding, glittering mermaid. You look around and you notice that you are attracting a herd of whales. They swim close to you and you jump on their backs, slide down their tails, and you swim around to look into their eyes with presence and reverence. You talk to the whales nonverbally and let them know that you are so happy they have joined you on this journey. You swim ahead of them and they follow you. You spend a playful time in the ocean connecting with them, while being in pure bliss.

You may think this is silly, but when the women come out of this meditation, they are radiant and lit from within. They are more connected to their joy and feel more in their pleasure and magnetism. Bringing this type of play into your business not only keeps it fun, but it also opens up your team to be more receptive to the magic and miracles that life is made of. We all take business much too seriously, and often end up burning out as a result.

BLESS AND RECEIVE

In the Season of Awaken, we operate in a state of flow. In network marketing, this means that life supports us in connecting with those people we are meant to bless in a way that feels effortless. This doesn't mean we sit around all day waiting for people to knock on our door. What this means is that we are open, aware, watching, and listening for anyone the Universe puts into our field in any given moment.

Network marketing is attraction marketing. You get what you are. In this season you are connected to your pleasure and open to receiving—receiving the next conversation, receiving the next affiliate, and receiving the next steps to find success on your path.

When you are in receptive mode through being in your pleasure, you will find that serendipity occurs in your life in the most remarkable ways, and your business builds with greater ease.

Standing in line at the post office, the woman behind you will strike up a conversation. Within minutes you find you share common goals and she is the perfect person who wants to partner with you to build a business. You get a Facebook message from an old friend wanting to reconnect. You reach out and when they learn about your business they immediately say that they have been praying for something exactly like this.

I cannot tell you how many people have told me that joining this business with me has been the answer to their prayers. People all around you, right now, are praying for a way to make a change in their life, to help more people, to do something that means something, and to create more wealth and freedom for themselves and their families. We all have the incredible business opportunity our network marketing companies offer—which could be the answer to that prayer. The question is, "Will you bless their life by telling them about it?"

Network marketing is about gift-giving and blessing people's lives. Take a look at the questions you ask regarding your business. In Season of Discover we ask, "How can I find the next person to join my business?" In Season of Awaken we ask, "Whose life am I meant to bless today with my product, business opportunity, or community?" Two different questions, two different results.

GRATITUDE, GRATITUDE, GRATITUDE

Gratitude is the bridge between your desire and that desire manifested. People who have created massive success experience high levels of gratitude daily. Most people are living in the Season of Discover and focus on the problems. What you focus on grows. Focus on the problems and you get more of them. In Season of Awaken, we focus on gratitude for all of the beauty around us, even if there are parts of us that are suffering or stuck.

There is always something to be grateful for—even if that something is being alive and breathing. Start by focusing on the little things that you are grateful for daily. Even if you just have one person on your team so far, be so absolutely grateful for that person and the fact that your business is growing! Every day before I leave the house, or wherever it is that I happen to be staying, I say a prayer of gratitude thanking the Universe for connecting me with the perfect people that I am meant to partner with while I am out and about. I give thanks for all of the magic and miracles that I will be receiving and for all of the lives that I will be a blessing.

Be aware that when you focus on what you are grateful for it, you begin to attract more things to be grateful for into your life and business.

CREATING FROM PLEASURE

A Queen knows the art of creating from pleasure. When you connect with wombspace, hold the clear and specific vision of what you desire while you refuel with pleasure. See how deeply you can relax and surrender into the trust that these desires are on their way to you now. Have gratitude for these desires as if they are happening now in present time. Allow the pleasure (however you choose to invoke it) spread the feelings of ease, joy, relaxation, and energy throughout your body. Remember that in order to create something in your life, you must feel the emotions that you desire as a result of that item manifesting, *before* it actually comes into form. The more deeply you are able to feel the pleasure, surrender, and gratitude the more open you are to receive your desires.

I am still astonished at what manifests in my life after consciously doing this. The other evening, my partner and I chose to devote the entire evening to being in our pleasure. We did this in a variety of ways—eating, dancing, visioning, and deeply connecting to ourselves and each other. Throughout the evening, I would pause and connect to my wombspace, where I would hold my big vision of global expansion in a way that feels energized and fun within my business. I relaxed into this vision while feeling immense gratitude for it already happening. The next day I got a call from a seasoned network marketer on my team, who told me how excited he is that several leaders, in a country where we had just opened business, were ready to come on board and play big! Pleasure...it works every time ladies.

Before moving on to the next chapter, let me offer a quick recap. In the Season of Discover we must first be with the parts that need tending and attention. This gives us more energy to be able to get in touch with our desires. After we relax into the desire, without worrying about the how, we fuel that desire with pleasure and pour on self-love. This gets us into our power. Only then can we move into the next season, the Season of Transform, in which we create our most epic and extraordinary lives.

EXERCISE: REVELING IN THE PLEASURE

Sit in your wombspace connecting position. Close your eyes and place your hands, palm over palm, on your wombspace. Relax your shoulders and jaw and start to breathe and move your pelvis. Smile. With every breath feel more relaxed, energized, and present. Go into your temple.

The Season of Awaken is about slowing down. There is much magic in stillness and in *being*.

Slow your pelvic movement. Slow your breath and make each inhale and exhale intentional, breathing all the way into wombspace. Now, drop a cord from your wombspace down to the center of the earth. Feel the weight of gravity pulling you down. Feel your connection to the earth and the support and limitless energy she provides.

Move your hips in a circular motion or whatever rhythm and motion that feels most pleasurable. Really feel your hips and pelvis as they move. Enjoy it. Revel in it. Relax even more, deepen your breath, and feel the pleasure of slowing down. Feel the pleasure of being connected to your body and sensuality.

Send love and appreciation to every part of your body, especially the parts you judge. Visualize your receiving channels opening. See and feel a beautiful, golden, radiating light that starts in your wombspace and expands into the rest of your body. This light fills you, radiates outward, and makes you even more magnetic and attractive.

Relax into a state of trust and feel all of your desires moving toward you. Feel the feelings that you would feel if those desires were manifested now. Fuel with pleasure even more. Put a smile on your face. Stay with this for a few minutes. There is nothing more to do than to be present and feel good! The more you are able to access this place, the more your business will unfold with grace and ease.

To receive the bonus audio meditation that accompanies this chapter, visit: networkmarketingqueen.com.

JOURNAL: SOUL-ALIGNED MISSION AND PURPOSE

Write down your core desires. Then, write down your soul-aligned mission/purpose statement which comes from your core desires.

....

....

....

....

....

....

....

....

....

....

....

CHAPTER FOUR

CREATING: THE WILD WOMAN

"She remembered who she was and the game changed."
—LALAH DELIA

Have you ever felt so ready to take your power, passion, and courage back, so that you could make your dreams and desires a nonnegotiable?

Have you ever had so much energy moving through you that you were ready to say, "Thank you, but I no longer need you," to any thoughts, beliefs, patterns, or habits that no longer serve you?

Have you ever been so lit up and on fire that you were willing to do whatever it takes to get from where you were to where you desired to be?

This is the Season of Transform.

The Season of Transform begins with us being furious that we have given our power away, settled, and played small. We are angry that we didn't show up and say yes to the things we knew we deserved and desired. In this season we become aware of, acknowledge, and accept that anger, which is the first step towards experiencing progress and forward movement.

In Season of Transform, we pull out our sword, draw a line in the sand, take our power and passion back into our own hands, and harness the courage to cross that line, shouting, "Enough! I deserve more than this!"

This is a season of further reclaiming our wholeness and inviting every single part—the ugly, beautiful, dark, light, sad, happy, scared, and fearless—home. We are then guided to our soul-aligned next steps from a more integrated place.

In the Season of Transform, victory is the only option. We show up, take action, and do whatever it takes to make our biggest dreams and desires a reality. We are so ready and nothing can get in our way. It is in this season that we reclaim our *wild*.

BE WILD

I refer to a woman who is resourced in the Season of Transform as *wild*. This term has a variety of definitions: "Not domesticated or cultivated." "Living in a state of nature and not ordinarily tamed." "Not subject to restraint or regulation." "Passionately eager or enthusiastic." "Indicative of strong passion, desire, or emotion."[4]

To me, a woman in her wild is real, raw, expressive, creative, chaotic, bold, and unapologetic. She owns her beauty and confidence. She knows who she is, what she desires, and that she is worthy and deserving. Nothing gets in her way. She is the pure potential of passion. She says, "I am my own mapmaker. I live my life according to my rules. I take my life back." To be a Queen, you must embrace your wild.

BECOME UNAVAILABLE

You get what you're available for. To experience massive success, you must make yourself *unavailable* for anything other than what is in alignment with your deepest heart's desire around your business. It is of utmost importance that you release anything that is no longer serving you or preventing you from showing up in your fullest potential.

The Season of Transform requires you to be willing to get incredibly uncomfortable. You must harness your power, passion, and courage to make those phone calls, get on that stage, do the in-home presentations, and take action in ways that will lead to your success. You must also be

---

4   Quoted from the Merriam-Webster Dictionary.

willing to say "No" to anything that is not in alignment with where you are going in your business and life.

This can actually be the hardest part of your journey to success. I have had to say goodbye to several romantic partnerships, friendships, and patterns in my life that were keeping me stuck. Each one of those goodbyes came with tremendous pain. Making the choice to let go of something that may be safe or comfortable, in order to grab onto what is in greater alignment with you and where you are going, can be excruciating. I literally thought I would die when my relationship with the father of my only child ended. I had to harness the courage and own my power consciously every single day to get through that time, knowing that by accepting the extreme level of uncertainty I was feeling, I would find freedom.

And the day I broke down on the kitchen floor, five years later, in another one of my darkest moments, was the day I made the decision and commitment that I would never be broke or sick again. That commitment was the beginning of me being energetically unavailable to not having money or being unwell in my body. I had to align myself to a path of wealth and health, which I continue to commit to every single day.

MAKE THE COMMITMENT

When I first joined my network marketing company I had a welcome call with our lead marketer. He asked me what I was excited about and why I said yes to joining. I heard myself share with him my big vision for myself and my life— parts of which I had never heard myself say! I also told him that I was going to be one of the top earners in the company and that he should keep his eye on me. I knew this was a moment to really show up and make these declarations to him and myself. Everything I shared on that call is now a reality. I had a clear vision and made the commitment and decision to do whatever it would take to get there, no matter what.

I will continue to reiterate the importance of committing and recommitting daily. Some people make a decision, commit to it one time, and then their focus wanders. A week or a month later, they are no longer committed. To be successful in life you have to make your decisions every single day. This requires, first, becoming aware of the real feelings that are present and acknowledging them, so that they don't unconsciously sabotage your business. Then, you must refocus on your true desires and fuel those desires with pleasure. This helps you become more receptive, magnetic, and attractive. Again, neuroscience shows us that pleasure plus self-love creates a "pleasure cocktail" that reroutes the pathways in your brain. This supports you to be more motivated, inspired, goal-oriented, and action-oriented. It also gets you into your power so that you can make the decisions that will create massive success in your life.

So, I support you to commit. Every day, make the commitment to build a thriving organization, reach your desired rank, make a certain amount of money, and most importantly, bless a certain number of lives. Make these nonnegotiables in your life.

People think that showing up fully, being in action, and playing a big game will take too much energy. Because of this, most people stay small. The truth is that playing small is exhausting. It takes so much more energy to stay stuck than to play a big game in a way that is aligned with our soul mission and purpose. When we do what we love, share our gifts, and serve others, we are fueled with endless energy.

BE FIERCE, WITH LOVE

You are the mama bear of your team and you love your people fiercely. Winning in network marketing requires you to sometimes say to them what nobody else has the courage to say. You must give honest feedback and reflection when you see something that may be blocking your team member's success. Before providing this feedback it is always good to ask, "Can I give you some feedback and tell you what I see?" Get their permission and then be honest and real.

I have conversations with people on my team when they wonder why their team is not growing or why nobody is doing anything. I am not afraid to lovingly point out the things that may be holding them back. Maybe they don't show up to company calls or haven't stepped up into true leadership yet. I ask them whether or not they have made the decision to succeed and if they are truly committed. I also ask them what they think the block is so that I can help them get to the other side. I then support them to commit to discontinuing certain patterns, habits, or toxic relationships that may be hindering their success. I am bold in the way that I am so real with my team when it comes to helping them truly understand what it takes to transform their business and life. I do this because I want them to win. Winning in this business takes consistency, persistence, determination, and commitment and we must repeatedly communicate that to our people in a powerful and passionate way.

Being bold with each other, in service to each other, is actually one of the things I love most about this industry. There is the potential for us to experience radical personal growth when we receive feedback from those who are courageous enough to give it to us because they want us to thrive.

So many women play the role of the "sweet, nice, good girl." You will never win in network marketing or in life if you are always sweet and accommodating. When you are truly the wild woman, living in the Season of Transform, you take your power back and unapologetically get fierce with your team, with all of the love in the world. One of the biggest gives you can give them is being brave enough to say the things that nobody else will.

REVERENCE AND RESPECT

Your business is sacred. Network marketing requires focus and needs to be treated as much more than a side hustle. You can't just show up once in a while and expect to be massively successful. You have to decide to be present, dive in with your entire being, and give your business the respect and reverence that it deserves.

Set your schedule and stick to it. This doesn't mean you have to work every day or even every week, but make sure you give your network marketing business attention, time, and focus. Many people who participate in network marketing view it as a part-time or side job. That is okay if your goals are limited, but if you want to build a massively successful business and create a legacy, you have to view it as much more and do the daily work and rituals that are required to win here in a big way.

DAILY RITUALS

Succeeding in network marketing, and anywhere in life, requires consistent daily rituals. Your daily rituals will be unique to you and will act as fuel to your success fire. We all know that as successful businesswomen, we travel and are often not in the same daily routine. Do the best you can with these rituals and commit to doing them at least five to six times a week, no matter where you are and what your schedule entails. This *will* change your business. The following daily rituals have been instrumental in creating the massive success that I have experienced in my business and life.

MEDITATION

Each morning I sit in my infrared sauna and meditate for twenty minutes. (If you don't have a sauna, meditate in a quiet place where you will not be disturbed.) I connect with my wombspace and activate it with my breath and movement, just as we did in the exercise in the previous chapter. I go into my temple with my guides and take inventory of any parts that may be in the Season of Discover that need acknowledgment and acceptance. I then feel and receive a golden light washing over my head and down my entire body, lighting me up and fueling me with a connection to something larger than myself.

I then focus on gratitude and find three things in my business and personal life that I am grateful for. I picture my life three years ahead and see what my relationships, business, energy, and health look like. I see myself in the future, living that life and feeling the emotions that are present as a result of having a life that I am wild and crazy about. I then envision the day ahead and, in my mind, walk through any upcoming conversations or interactions that I will have around my business. I see these happening in present time and view them as being easy, energized, and fun. You can't create what you can't imagine, see, and feel!

Next, I get into my pleasure through smiling or moving my hips and feeling my body breathing and becoming more alive. I feel my receiving channels open and I allow myself to be more magnetic and attractive, so that my destiny can come towards me with a greater sense of effortlessness.

I then pour on the self-love and let the "pleasure cocktail" activate my power, so I can boldly say my mantras out loud. One of my favorite mantras currently is, "I am a joyful, soulful, international, millionaire wife." I got this from the book *Leveraging the Universe* by Mike Dooley and I added "wife" on the end because it was time to upgrade the old version of me that had been a single mother for way too long.

I also use the ultimate success mantra from *The Big Leap* by Gay Hendricks, which is, "I expand in abundance success, and love every day, and inspire others to do the same." I then say my money mantra from *Think and Grow Rich* by Napoleon Hill (which I will explain further in chapter five) with power, passion, and energy.

BOOKS/AUDIOS

After my meditation, I either read or listen to audiobooks for at least fifteen minutes. These books are typically on the topics of wealth consciousness and personal growth (you can find a list of recommended reading in the appendix).

Reading books and listening to audios on topics around which you need to grow is critical to your success. I encourage you to do the same, for at least fifteen minutes every morning and every evening. This is a must!

JOURNALING

I journal daily for ten to fifteen minutes a day, writing out the vision for my life as if it is happening *now*, similar to what I picture during my meditation. Journaling closes the gap between where you are and where you desire to be. When I journal, I get very specific. My favorite thing to journal is "As the woman who makes X amount of money each month, I am…(This is where I write down how I am feeling, the actions I am taking, where I'm traveling to, and what my life looks like.)" I journal as if everything is happening in real time.

GOAL SETTING

It is key to set goals and know exactly where you are headed. Know the exact dollar amount you desire (and ultimately *choose*) to be making and how you can get there with your specific company. Know your compensation plan and your criteria for the next rank so you are focused on those specific numbers. Hold those numbers in your vision and mind every day. Write them on sticky notes that you place around the house. Speak and write as if you have already made that rank and earned that level of income. If you don't know where you are going, you will never get there. I am a big fan of thirty-day, ninety-day, and six-month goals.

CONSCIOUS LANGUAGE

This is probably the most important factor in determining whether or not you will be successful in your business! Your words create your reality. I want to support you to always use conscious language. Don't say you *want* something; say you *desire* it. *Want* is actually a lack word and serves to keep that thing that you want outside of yourself. When you use the word *desire*, you are more able to feel it already as a part of yourself, which brings it closer to you. Don't use the word *can't*. Don't say you are broke, or that something is hard, or that there is not enough. You would be amazed to know how often you actually use words of lack throughout your day. Say, "I can! I must! There is enough!" Ask the people closest to you to hold you accountable to only use conscious language. Make this part of the culture of your team.

EXERCISE

I exercise at least six days a week. It's our job to light our own fire and get ourselves in the energy of transform every single day. Exercise gets your blood flowing and energy moving so that you can do what is required to win. Exercise is crucial for you to feel good in your body and mind, which is key to experiencing massive success.

SELF-CARE

Self-care is an invaluable daily habit. Every day we must take impeccable care of ourselves. Sit in a sauna, take a walk in nature, meditate, take a hot bath, get a massage, and eat healthy. Get at least eight to nine hours of sleep each night, especially during the hours of 10:00 p.m. to 2:00 a.m. These are ways to nourish and care for ourselves and they are necessary for experiencing success in your business in a way that is sustainable and energized.

PLEASURE

Daily pleasure breaks are crucial! Remember, pleasure opens your receiving channels so that you can let in all of the desires that you have decided on. Spend five to ten minutes a few times a day lying in the sun, taking a quick nap, having a short dance party, or doing whatever puts you in your feel-good place. This is one of the keys to success in your business, as we have been talking about throughout this whole book!

DAILY ACTION STEPS WITHIN YOUR NETWORK MARKETING BUSINESS

Along with your daily rituals, there are daily actions that are integral to the growth of your business. Author and network marketing expert, Eric Worre, believes the following seven skills are fundamental to your success—and I like to include an eighth:

1. Finding New Prospects
2. Inviting
3. Presenting
4. Follow-Up
5. Closing
6. Plugging into the System and Training
7. Promoting Events
8. Staying Organized and Connected to Your Team/Building a Team Culture

Most people in this industry know of these skills and go about them in a certain way. As a woman building my business according to the principles that I'm sharing with you in this book, I implement these skills in a different manner than most. I connect with my wombspace to get resourced with the pleasure, power, wisdom, courage, and intuition that allows me to carry out each skill in a way that is more energized and fun. Remember, connection with wombspace changes everything!

FINDING NEW PROSPECTS

Remember, network marketing is about thinking big! You don't want to just find new prospects. You want to be very intentional with your prospecting and ultimately find influencers who are well connected, community driven, independent, and coachable. (That said, you never know who may turn into an influencer and it's a good idea to stay open to the people the Universe puts in your field and see their greatest potential.)

You are magnetic, radiant, and attractive, and are *only* available to work with people who are driven, focused, and committed. You attract rock stars with great wealth consciousness, who are team players, energetic, and fun to work with. This is attraction marketing and remember, you attract who you are. If you are attracting people who aren't showing up the way you would like them to, it's time to look at how you are showing up. Become the woman that is your ideal team member.

When I am in my morning meditation and am envisioning the day ahead, I connect with my wombspace and say, "Thank you for magnetizing to me the perfect people who are ready to be blessed by our products and the business. Thank you for helping me open to receive business partners who are well connected, positive, coachable, fun to work with, and ready to create a wildly successful business and life. Thank you for putting them in my path and for helping me recognize them." I also always ask, "Whose life can I bless through these products and business opportunity today?" I am often shown a face or name. I always trust this. Your wombspace is your place of infinite wisdom and always knows.

When you do your meditation, I suggest you define the exact number of influencers you would like to connect with over the next month. From your place of power, make this a nonnegotiable, and be open to receiving. Listen for the next aligned steps and then take action.

INVITING

Once the Universe has put these people in your path, you must have the courage to move forward and invite. To win in this industry, you must harness your power, be willing to get uncomfortable, and be okay with people saying *no*. Many times *no* means *not yet* and after you follow up with more information and support, that *no* will turn into a *yes*. If it is a hard *no*, remember: SW, SW, SW, SW (Some will, some won't, so what, someone's waiting!)

When it comes to inviting, be bold. Invite prospects to a presentation, a three-way call, an in-home presentation, or to view a video you will send them. Make it about serving them, and not about you.

Remember, connecting with your wombspace, knowing

your desire, and then getting into your pleasure and self-love ignites your power and your ability to be confident, empowered, and able to take bold action towards doing the things that you are afraid of.

PRESENTING

This is a scary one for most people! I know it was for me when I first started. Prior to every presentation, I do my wombspace-connecting meditation. I ask to be an open channel to bless all of the people in the room with whatever it is they need. The more I can get out of my way and be purely of service, the more effortless the message comes through and the more fun I have. Now, I love presenting.

And, it's okay to be scared! Fear is part of the process. Remember, done is better than perfect. Make mistakes. Say something wrong. It's okay. Take your power back, be willing to be uncomfortable, and do it—even if it scares you. If you wait to be perfect, you're never going to win...here or anywhere else in life. The more you present, the easier it will be. You can also present with other team members, or even people cross team in your area, and you'll feel a greater level of support and ease.

FOLLOW UP

Remember, there is nothing more feminine than connection and community—both of which are integral to success in network marketing. After your presentation, you need to foster connection by following up.

Harness your power and courage and reach out. Ask what your prospect liked about what they heard and if they have any questions. I love the 2/2/2 rule. Follow up with them two days after you did a presentation or sent them a video. If they are not ready to enroll, follow up two weeks after the event, and then two months after if they have still not enrolled. Remember, it usually takes between three to seven touches before someone will say yes and be ready to join your team. Add them to your database so you can continue to connect, reach out, and nurture the relationship by adding value to their lives.

I literally touched one of my biggest builders ten to fifteen times before she said yes. At one point she even blocked me on her phone, but I didn't let that stop me. I knew she was meant to do this and as a result of me continuing to follow up, and her finally saying yes, her entire life has changed. She is a single mother of three children and is now experiencing much more ease and freedom in her life.

You can always say to someone, "I am going to keep connecting with you around these life-changing products and incredible business opportunity until you tell me to leave you alone!" Be honest, upfront, and let them know that they have permission to tell you to stop reaching out.

CLOSING

Again, ask your prospect what they liked about the presentation or video you sent them. Ask if they have any questions and answer them or get connected on a three-way call with your upline if you need support. Remember, you are not alone! That is the beauty of this industry, we do it *together* and support each other to win. But you must know how to ask for support and receive it.

Many women shy away from asking the final question to close, "How would you like to get started?" This can require a greater level of harnessing your power, but remember, you can also make it light and fun! It doesn't need to be so heavy. Say things like, "Do you want to join our community? Are you ready to play? Do you want to do it? Are you excited to move forward with creating the freedom and success that you desire?"

PLUGGING INTO THE SYSTEM AND TRAINING

When I first started network marketing, it was critical for me to find a fun and energized way to keep people connected with my community, and to train and educate my team. For each of you, this will look different. You must first know your desire around your team culture. What is your team name? What is the mission and purpose of your team? Connect to wombspace to receive guidance and help you get clarity. Remember, wombspace is your place of infinite wisdom.

It is so important to have the ability to plug your people into good systems and structures in order to better leverage your time. Every company has overarching systems in place to help you and your team grow. As women desiring to make six or seven figures in this industry, we must support our team members in feeling connected and supported. The number one reason why people don't stay in a company is because they don't feel loved or cared for enough. Network marketing gives us women the opportunity to do what we do best all day long...love on and care for people. All my new team members are welcomed into a Facebook group so they can feel part of the community. I also connect them to a WhatsApp group where we post upcoming calls, trainings, and flyers for events around the world.

Remember: don't go into management mode. In network marketing, 70 to 80 percent of your time should be making connections, building your team through recruiting, plugging in, and training new people. Only 20 to 30 percent of your time should be spent on greater team training.

PROMOTING EVENTS

It is so important to always promote events. Whether these are small in-home presentations, bigger events in your community, or company conventions—events are the key to building your business. Our society is becoming more technology-driven and less connected, and people have a hunger to come together in the flesh. One of the things I love most about this industry is the ability for people to feel part of something bigger where they are heard, seen, valued, and supported.

Connect with your wombspace to determine what kind of events fuel you the most in building your business. Notice how you are guided to move. What has the most energy? One-on-one's at a coffee shop? Serving drinks and appetizers before your in-home presentation? Renting a fabulous space downtown for a more luxurious feel to your event?

One woman on my team is an incredible musician. At the beginning of her events, she plays a song or two to connect with her radiance and magnetism. She then feels more alive and energized as she moves into her presentation. The people who attend are fed by her music and are then more open to receive the information on the products and business opportunity. I have another woman on my team who is a DJ. We have done events where we share the products with people during her DJ set after the presentation.

When we bring in more of who we are, and more of what we love to our events, people become more attracted, energized, and compelled to want what it is that we have.

Remember, there is nothing more feminine than connection and community, and events are a way to keep us fueled and lit up while we build.

STAYING ORGANIZED AND CONNECTED TO YOUR TEAM, AND BUILDING A TEAM CULTURE

In Season of Transform, you are the *creatrix*. This is *your* team and you can paint the blank canvas of your business in any way you want. What do you want your team to represent? What's the culture of your team? Do you have weekly parties or gatherings online or in person? How are you all connected? Is it through a Facebook group or a WhatsApp chat? In network marketing you get to play, have fun, and create a compelling culture for your team. Remember, people come for the product or opportunity, but stay for the culture and community. Perhaps you want to stay connected with daily or weekly Facebook Lives on your team page. Maybe before each big company convention, you host an event for your team only. Again, the more you are connected to your wombspace, the more connected you are to what really lights you up in your business.

Celebration is a big part of how we see and support each other. Celebrating the people in your company is key to creating a culture that people are proud to be a part of. Publicly recognize people as they achieve rank or goals. Let them know how valued they are. Make it a priority to help them feel connected and part of the community.

Network marketing only stays energized and joyful when you're giving your gifts within your company and your team. On Tuesdays I host a coaching call for my team because that is a gift I can offer and love to share. If I couldn't give my gifts within this company, I would quit. Money is just money. Real joy comes from sharing our gifts and living in alignment with our souls' deepest callings.

I also do a weekly Zoom to support the women on my team to build their business from their feminine power. The women are often amazed that they get this free resource. They joined an incredible company, receive free coaching and guidance on how to transform their lives, while they are helping people and making money at the same time! I've created a rich team culture that adds significant value to people's lives, which is an important part of how I got to seven figures in less than two years.[5]

Now, you may not be a life coach or have a passion around guiding your women in the way that I do—and that is absolutely fine. You have your own unique gifts that you bring to your team. We *all* have gifts to give and the beautiful thing about network marketing is that we get to be curious about what those gifts are and then bring them forth into the world.

---

[5] Again, there are never any promises or guarantees of income in network marketing. You may not make any money or you may make six or seven figures!

HAVING IT ALL

Again, playing small is exhausting. When we make the choice to play a bigger game, have incredible impact, show up in our fullness, make the decision to have it all, and then move in action to create our most extraordinary lives, we are so fully fueled, inspired and lit up.

In the Season of Transform, a woman decides that she can be, do, and have whatever it is that she desires. She can have it all—optimal health and wellness, an exquisite partnership and other extraordinary relationships, an incredible community, a rich spiritual life, a career that she loves so much that she never wants to retire, and an infinite supply of money to live her life of freedom and contribution.

This is all possible for you. It is possible for every woman.

In order to experience massive success in network marketing, we must make the decision to change our relationship with money. This is a significant topic we are now ready to explore. In the next chapter we will discuss money in all of the Seasons of Well-Being and how you can become an open channel for money to endlessly and abundantly flow to and through you.

EXERCISE: HARNESSING YOUR POWER

Sit in your wombspace connection position. Close your eyes and place your hands, palm over palm, over your wombspace. Relax your shoulders and jaw. Activate your wombspace with breath and movement. See yourself in your temple, feeling relaxed, energized, and aligned.

Get in touch with your desires. These desires can be more general, such as the desire to be of higher-level service to others, to make more money, or to have a greater level of freedom in your life. Then get specific about the desires and action steps that will lead you to these more general desires. This may involve giving a great presentation, having your first three-way call, recruiting a specific number of people, reaching a new rank, etc. Just be with these desires and relax into them without worrying about the *how*.

Connect with your pleasure through pelvic movement and breath, and your connection to the earth. Feel yourself being held, supported, and loved by the Great Mother that the earth is. Rest into this precious connection with yourself and with her. Let yourself become even more relaxed and energized. Let self-love wash over your entire being, remembering to saturate even the parts of you that you don't love. Let this pleasure and self-love, and the resulting "pleasure cocktail," ignite your power, passion, and courage. Feel a fire burning in your wombspace and let that fire spread throughout your entire body. Take out your sword and see yourself drawing a line in the sand. Feel how ready you are to cross over that line to reclaim your desires, your business, and your life.

Feel your spine in alignment as you allow the energy of this power, passion, and courage to move into every cell. Use this energy to make your desires a nonnegotiable. Make a decision and a commitment that you are unavailable for anything else.

Now, bring in a Creating Guide. This being, just like your Healing Guide can be a teacher or mentor in your life, a Goddess, a power animal, etc. Most importantly she is powerful and loving. See her as an ally and someone that fully supports you in creating your business. Know that she has your back, wants you to be massively successful, and is able to guide you when it comes to creating. Ask her for your next aligned action steps that will support you in having your desires. Listen for the answers. Thank your Creating Guide for her support and guidance.

Write down the next aligned action steps that you received and then use this burning fire of passion and power to go out and boldly build your business. Remember, it is our responsibility to light our own fires each and every day so that we can create our most fulfilling lives.

To receive the bonus audio meditation that accompanies this chapter, visit: networkmarketingqueen.com.

CHAPTER FIVE

READY FOR A RED HOT LOVE AFFAIR?

"Money is not the most important thing in the world. Love is. Fortunately, I love money."

—JACKIE MASON

How would it feel to know that you can, without a shadow of a doubt, have all the money you desire?

What would it be like to have a hot, fun, energized relationship with money in which you knew you were unconditionally loved, supported, and taken care of?

I loooove talking about money. Trust me...it definitely wasn't always this way. As I mentioned before, I was once extremely broke and sick and was quickly losing my will to keep going. I came to a crossroads and knew I had to go one of two ways. I could continue being a victim—stuck in my blame and suffering—or I could take my power back and say *yes* to living a life that I would be madly in love with on all levels. It may seem silly and as if everyone would obviously choose the latter, but I want to be clear about something...

There comes a time in our lives, perhaps several times, when we come to a crossroads and are faced with making a choice around how we move forward. It would seem as though everyone would make the choice to reclaim their power and create an incredible life, right? Unfortunately, most people have no idea how to do this. By default, they choose to stay stuck in their suffering. Harnessing feminine power is a high art and one that we as women have been disconnected from for way too long. We *always* have a choice in life. The key is knowing how to own your power so that you can make the decision that will ultimately lead to a limitless amount of joy, abundance, and connection.

Living from your feminine power and creating an extraordinary life requires making the decision to change your relationship with money. Many years ago, I made it my job to change my relationship with money. I spent several hours each and every day on this mission, and what I experienced was truly incredible. The more resourced I got with money, the healthier I became and the more energy I had to be me. Why did this happen? Because money is simply energy—an energy that fuels us to be who we are. Most people hate talking about money because they have a terrible relationship with it. But let's be real. We all need to get down with money on a much deeper level.

The number one block I see around people not succeeding in network marketing is their belief in their stories around money. This chapter is key to your success because when you transform your relationship with money, the world is your oyster.

As I've discussed in talking about the Seasons of Well-Being, the key to freedom and success is being aware of, acknowledging, and accepting the season in which you currently reside. From there, you can consciously call in more of the season in which you need to be, so that you can grow and thrive. We will now explore the experience of money in each of these seasons so that you will better see where you are and what is possible. In which season do you live when it comes to money? Which season do you need more of? Remember, awareness is key!

MONEY AND THE SEASON OF DISCOVER

When it comes to money, most women (and men for that matter) are in the Season of Discover and feel helpless, hopeless, and in fear that their money problems will never end. They feel like there is never going to be enough of it and that they have to work *so* hard to grasp even just a little of it, only to have it slip away with the smallest gust of wind.

In this season, you feel defeated, frustrated, and stuck, like you're on a gerbil wheel that's moving at top speed, working so hard with no breakthrough in sight. Money seems so elusive, and only the elite have it. You watch them spend their cash lavishly on vacations, homes, cars, nice clothing, and expensive spa treatments. You feel jealous and may even start to hate money and your relationship with it.

Here's the key—in the Season of Discover, you're still a victim and everything is happening *to* you. You forgot that you have a choice. It's okay that you forgot, and there will be a time soon to remember that you can have as much money as you desire, but now it's time to get real about what is! At this *very* moment I want you to become aware of exactly where you are when it comes to money. Ask yourself the following questions.

- Do you refuse to talk about money?
- Are you deathly afraid of money?
- Do you feel like you're always in survival mode or barely have enough to make it through the month?
- Does your body tense up when you think about money?
- Do you feel powerless when it comes to money?
- Do you feel afraid that having money will change you?

- Do you feel helpless, exhausted, and defeated when it comes to money?
- Do you feel frustrated and stuck around money?

Now, put your hands on your body over an area of tension or pain—as this is usually where the emotions that are associated with your money stories are anchored. Acknowledge what is true for you around money, without trying to change it. Allow and accept these emotions and parts of yourself.

Perhaps you feel money has forgotten you or passed you by. Maybe you feel unsupported and unloved by money. Let that childlike part of you have a voice. Allow, acknowledge, and breathe into this place within you. Hear what these parts have to say. Send them love, remembering that the more you accept them, the less they are able to run you and your life.

Most people avoid these emotions and parts of themselves like the plague, because they are just too painful to feel. But what we resist persists. This is part of why people have never-ending money issues. You have to get to the core of the feelings and emotions that are true for you regarding money. Feel them. Express them through voice or movement. Scream, yell, cry, or maybe just lie on the floor, balled into a heap of hopelessness. When you can fully be with something, there is also automatically less charge. This makes room for more energy to be available for you to move into the Season of Transform and take your power back.

MONEY AND THE SEASON OF TRANSFORM

In the Season of Transform you take back your power, passion, and courage in order to create your deepest desires regarding money. Money is a choice and a decision. It is simply our birthright. It is an energy that has the potential to flow to and through us all the time, so that we can be more energized to give our gifts in service to others and live to our fullest potential.

My life did not change until I said, "Never again will I only have enough! Never again will I suffer when it comes to money! Never again will I feel drained in my relationship with money!" I made the decision, drew a line in the sand, and fiercely crossed over it. I made the choice that my relationship with money would be fun and energized. I knew money would be available for me, support me, and that it would show up unconditionally for me. I could have as much money moving through me as I desired at any given moment.

You get what you allow yourself to be available for. I made myself only available to know myself as a money magnet. That is when the money started flowing and it hasn't stopped since.

CHANGING YOUR BELIEFS AROUND MONEY

If you don't have enough money flowing through your life, it is because you continue to carry negative beliefs about it. You believe that there is not enough money, that you are not worthy, that it is bad to have money, that money will change you, or that it's not there for you unconditionally.

Your beliefs create your life. In the Season of Transform you take a look at your beliefs and then change the ones that aren't serving you. I know I am making this sound easy, but this takes practice. You can't just *say*, "I can have as much money as I desire." You have to *believe* those words. On a daily basis, speak your new beliefs regarding money. This will result in your subconscious mind believing that they are true. Marilyn Jenett, in her book *Feel Free to Prosper*, says that the conscious mind and the subconscious mind must agree in order for the desire to manifest. She says that the conscious mind is like the male and the subconscious mind is like the female and when they merge and unite (make love), they produce children, which are the desires. Doing the daily inner work around money is like impregnating the subconscious—which I think is brilliant.

So what are your new beliefs around money?

- The more money I make, the more generous I can be.
- The more money I make, the more energy I have and the more gifts I can give back.

- The more money I make, the more powerful I am and the more I can create true change in the world.
- I am an open channel for money to flow to and through— endlessly and abundantly.
- Money loves me, and I love money.
- I can attract as much money as I desire to me now.
- I get paid to do nothing.

Reflect on that last point. *You get paid to do nothing.* Most people believe they must work sixty hours a week to make the money they desire, so they don't even bother to try. They believe it's too hard and too much, so they settle for their current reality when it comes to money.

I currently get paid to do nothing. I get paid while I sleep. I get paid while I'm playing in the ocean on vacation with my daughter. I get paid as I am taking a nap in the sun in the middle of the day. Please, don't get me wrong! I show up fully every single day for my team and the people I love, and it's not always a walk in the park or a nap in the sun. But what we are talking about here is *passive income.* We play full out, build our communities, support them, and get paid while we sleep. And the best thing is that the more we get paid the more we are helping others with our products and opportunity. This is the beautiful thing about network marketing!

LIGHTING YOUR FIRE

The more I am in my pleasure, the more money I earn. When I am relaxed and energized, money flows through me.

I'm sure you're asking *how do I do that?* How do I bring myself into greater pleasure? Into greater peace? Into greater energy? Into greater joy? Into greater gratitude? Into greater relaxation?

In Season of Transform we embrace these emotions now, *before* we have the money. We feel peace, relaxation, gratitude, ease, and joy just because we are alive. In this Season, we take our power back and light our own fire in order to feel the emotions we think money will bring us—right now. We do this by doing the things that help us get in touch with these emotions—hiking in nature, being with people that we love, meditating, mantras, and, of course, connecting to wombspace. We must also get into alignment so that our brains can reorganize and support us to authentically feel these feelings. Chiropractic, hemp extract, and any other practices that support your nervous system are crucial.

DOING WHAT IT TAKES

In Season of Transform, we engage in daily rituals such as saying our personal money mantra (we will create this at the end of this chapter!), doing our money meditation (available in the appendix), journaling, reading books, and listening to audios. The more you put attention toward changing your beliefs around money through these tools, the faster your subconscious will be "impregnated" and the faster your desires will be translated into reality.

In Season of Transform the key is to get specific. How much money are you choosing to make each month? A great place to start is to double your current income and then double it again. What if this was your new normal? If you had this much money coming in every month consistently, what would you be doing? Of course, during the first month you might choose to lay on the beach all day and refill your cup (in more ways than one), but we can only luxuriate on vacation for so long. True joy comes from giving our gifts in service to others. If you were making this much money, what actions would you take? What emotions would you feel? How much energy would flow through your body? How would you be more generous? What would be different in your life?

Do you want to know the difference between those of you who will succeed and those who won't? The ones who take the time to write those questions down, journal the answers as if they are true now, and do this with consistency, will be the ones who move on to be successful. We so often know *what* to do to get where we want to be, but don't actually make those steps nonnegotiable and *do* what it takes.

In Season of Transform, deep in our bones, we know that

we are meant to live an incredible life, while having great impact. If you don't feel that deep inside you, speak the following mantra every day:

I have an incredible life, serving others at a high level and making as much money as I desire, easily and effortlessly.

Remember, this is a decision. Decide right now that you are the woman who shows up in a way that inspires people to be around you. Decide right now that you always have more than enough money to live your most extraordinary life. Decide that money can be easy. Decide that you will never struggle again in regard to money. And remember, decision is a practice and needs to be made every single day. And, if there is not enough energy moving through you to make these decisions—go do something *now* that will light your fire and get you in the necessary state to make the decisions that will change your life.

MONEY AND MEN

Often the stories women have around men (or women if that is your sexual orientation) and love are the same stories they have around money. There is a strong correlation between the two. Let's think about some of your possible current beliefs around money. *Money is hard to get. It comes, but it never stays. It is conditional. There's never enough. I have to work really hard to get it, and I'm left feeling exhausted and overwhelmed. I don't feel loved or supported by money.* Do any of those ring true when it comes to men as well?

Luckily, these beliefs can change! The above thoughts don't have to be your narrative. When I knew, without a shadow of doubt, that money is unconditional and supports me, that it is easy and fun, that it loves me, that it flows to me endlessly, and that it is always available to me...that is when I attracted my current partner, and one of the most incredible men I have ever known, into my life. And I know, also without a shadow of a doubt, that he is unconditional in his love for me, supports me, and that our relationship is exciting and fun. Life gets really fun when we have extraordinary relationships with both money and men. Every Queen has her King! That said, there is divine timing around this, and sometimes a Queen just needs to be patient, continue to do her inner work, and love herself unconditionally while she waits for the King who is worthy of her to arrive. I could write a whole other book about this, but back on track...

Money is simply energy. It is not good, it is not bad. Where attention goes, energy flows, and money loves to be paid attention to. **Money is our birthright and we can make as much of it as we desire**, but it takes a conscious effort to transform our relationship with money to make it one that feels really alive and exciting.

One of my favorite ways to do this is by creating a Money

Honey, a concept conceived by Morgana Rae, teacher, speaker, and author of *Financial Alchemy*. Your Money Honey is a visual representation of money as a physical person—a man or a woman depending on your sexual orientation. Your Money Honey will be a desirable being with whom you will have a hot love affair. Your Money Honey unconditionally supports you, cherishes you, loves you, and will give you anything you ask for. He (I will use this pronoun so as not to be too wordy) is here to serve you.

You will begin a relationship with this being and pay attention to him every single day. When you first sit in your imagination with your Money Honey, let him know that you desire to have a fun, energized, and easy relationship with him. At first you may need to have some conversations with your Money Honey and acknowledge that you have some anger, doubt, fear, and sadness around your current relationship with him. But as you develop a deeper connection and trust, your relationship will transition to one that is fun, playful, and sexy. Like a lover, money loves to be wooed in a delightful way. It may take some time, but as this connection grows, allow yourself to relax and let go. Maybe dance for—or with—your Money Honey when you are with him. Be playful. Have fun. Let your imagination run wild, allowing yourself to experience the joy that this connection brings.

At the end of this chapter you will create your Money Honey

and begin this newfound connection which will become invaluable in your life.

KEEP IT SEXY

Many of us are disconnected from our sensuality because we've been culturally conditioned to believe being sexy is wrong, and that if we own our feminine power, we will be judged, attract negative attention, and possibly find ourselves in harmful situations. We fear that being more feminine will result in us losing our power, but the opposite is true. Our sensuality and sexuality *are* so much of our power, when harnessed the right way.

In his book *Think and Grow Rich*, author Napoleon Hill discusses the mystery of sex transmutation. Hill says that people who are very successful are highly sexed. The "sex desire" is the most powerful of human desires, and when it is harnessed and redirected, this motivating force can morph into a powerful creativity that drives success and thus helps one accumulate riches.

When we get into our wombspace, our pelvis, our sensuality, and our sexuality, we can channel this energy into a potent force of creation. Wombspace is the space where life is created. The energy here is endless, and we can channel it directly into wealth and success in our network marketing business.

To me, sexy is radiance. It is shining your inner light to bless everyone you are around. It is owning your power and showing up unapologetically as the beautiful, powerful human being that you are. It is being in alignment so that there is limitless energy moving through you in any given moment. It is knowing yourself as the love that you are, and inspiring others to remember that within themselves. It is owning the perfection of your God-given body and feeling at home in it. When we feel sexy, we feel alive and are better able to tap into our creativity and make our dreams a reality when it comes to money and everything else.

So, keep it sexy. This doesn't mean flaunting your sexuality around other people or having no boundaries. It means connecting with the deep and sensual part of yourself that owns her power and uses it for the good of all.

MONEY AND THE SEASON OF AWAKEN

In this season, there's nothing much to do! In the Season of Awaken, money feels effortless and you have a deep faith and trust in it. Money just flows endlessly and abundantly to and through you, because you know that it is your birthright. It's like saying, "The sun rises, the sun sets, and money is easy." It just is.

The Season of Awaken is a season where you feel connected to something bigger than yourself. The more you get energized and connected to this bigger thing through dance, yoga, meditation, nature, or being in a community that lights you up, the more you become a money magnet. In Season of Awaken, you deeply know your worth and the gifts that you bring to the world. Giving your gifts in service is number one. You know so deeply who you are and have mastered the art of self-love—which opens you up even more to the flow of money moving to and through you.

In the Season of Awaken money flows like breathing. You breathe in and you breathe out. Money is the same. It flows in and flows out. Remember, abundance is infinite and money is infinite. There is more than enough money for every single one of us.

In this season, we receive the money that flows in graciously and have gratitude for the money that flows out. Say *thank you* when you pay your bills. Feel proud when you donate to charity. The more money that flows out, the more money that flows in. Money comes effortlessly to you, especially when you are in your pleasure. Remember, desire is the wanting, pleasure is the receiving.

In the Season of Awaken, you trust that you are taken care of and supported unconditionally by money. Money wants you to have as much of it as you desire, so that you can give more of *you* with greater energy, passion, and purpose. A true Queen knows this to be so.

JOURNAL: MONEY HONEY

Describe your Money Honey in the space below. Get specific. What color hair does he (or she) have? How tall is he? What is his body type? What is he wearing? How does he feel? What is his presence like? His posturing? His facial expression? What does your relationship look and feel like?

....

....

....

....

....

....

EXERCISE: MONEY HONEY

Sit in your wombspace connecting position. Close your eyes and place your hands, palm over palm, on your wombspace. Relax your shoulders and your jaw and start activating this space with breath and movement as you have done in the previous chapters. Allow yourself to drop deeply into your pleasure.

See yourself in your temple, feeling how good it feels to be in this place of endless resource, energy, and nourishment. See and feel your Money Honey there with you. Be with him and let him know that you are so honored and excited to cultivate a loving and fun relationship with him. Feel your Money Honey loving, cherishing, and adoring you and giving himself over unconditionally to you. Be playful with your Money Honey. Dance for or with him. Now, increase your pleasure even more by smiling, circling your hips, stretching your body, or relaxing more deeply into your breath, and allow this to open you even more to the receiving.

Then, sit down and gaze into his eyes. Ask, "How am I meant to call more of you to me? Who do I need to be and what do I need to do in order for you to flow with more ease and grace to and through me so I can be of greater service to others? What are my next steps to being able to receive more of you?" Remember, we only get into action *after* we fuel our desires around money with pleasure.

Keep it a hot, sexy love affair. Remember, money loves to be paid attention to and wooed daily. Let your Money Honey know that you will be cultivating this relationship on an ongoing basis. Thank him for the unconditional flow of money that is always available to you.

 To receive the bonus audio meditation that accompanies this chapter, visit: networkmarketingqueen.com.

EXERCISE: IMPREGNATING THE SUBCONSCIOUS

Every day repeat the following conscious language statements around money:

- I can have as much money as I desire!
- I will have as much money as I desire!
- I choose to have as much money as I desire!
- I have as much money as I desire!
- I love having as much money as I desire!
- I create as much money as I desire!
- I enjoy as much money as I desire!

Repeat these statements, as well as your new beliefs around money, for at least thirty days. There is no way that your old money stories can survive when you focus on these new ones!

JOURNAL: NEW NONNEGOTIABLE

What is your current income level?

....

Double that number.

....

Now double that amount again.

This is your new normal and new nonnegotiable.

Now, journal the following: "As the woman who consistently, easily and effortlessly makes X amount of dollars (using the new nonnegotiable above), without question each and every month, I am...(who would you be, how would you feel, what would you be doing, and what does your life look like?)" Repeat daily.

JOURNAL: MONEY MANTRA

Creating my money mantra has been a total game changer. This mantra comes from chapter two of Napoleon Hill's *Think and Grow Rich*, one of the most important books ever written about money. I have modified the format a bit to be more in alignment with building from your feminine power.

First, you have to know your money goals and the specific amount of money you choose to bring in every month... down to the dollar. Be specific about the amount and the date by which you want to start having this money in your life. Only when you focus on the specifics of this energy does it really begin to move through you. The beginning of the mantra is easy!

"I choose to easily attract to me a minimum of *X dollars* a month by *Y date*."

Next, it's important to write down where the money will be spent. You have to know where every penny of that dollar amount is going to go because money loves to have a purpose. Through doing this, you will learn to pay attention to the energy flow of money. You can't just say you need $10,000. You need to know why you need it—such as $4,000 on rent and bills, $1,000 on food, $500 for your car, $500 on shopping or a weekend getaway. Don't only focus on your basic needs, but also add your deepest desires as well. Add $1,000 for a vacation, $400 for weekly massages or spa treatments, $500 a month to donate to a charity or cause you are passionate about, or whatever else makes your heart sing. Add in money for the tasks you need to delegate, like a nanny, a financial advisor, and a gardener. Money flows where there's a true desire, so make sure the desires are authentic and really light you up.

Once you've recorded your projected expenditures, it's important to determine the ways in which you will receive that money. Add a statement to your mantra that says something like, "I am receiving this money by building my network marketing business, enrolling ten new affiliates, any other streams of income you may have, and receiving money from unexpected sources." You want to be open to the endless channels from where the money can come. Since money is unlimited, and there is plenty of it in the world, it can truly come from anywhere.

Combined together, the mantra looks like the following:

"I choose to easily attract to me a minimum of x dollars each month, by ....(date)........ .

The purpose for this money is

....

I am receiving this money by/from

....

My faith is so strong that this money will be in my possession. I can now see it with my eyes and touch it with my hands. (Print out a money symbol and look at it, touch it, and woo it.) It is now awaiting transfer to me in the proportion that I deliver the service I intend to render in return for it!"

Weave your mantra into your Money Honey meditation. Connect to your wombspace and activate it with breath and movement. Go into your temple, connect to the earth, and get into your pleasure, which will allow your receiving channels to open. Bring in your Money Honey. Let the pleasure ignite the power. Remember, pleasure plus self-love neurochemically changes your brain so that you are more confident, empowered, and able to make your choices a nonnegotiable. State your money mantra with power and passion, believing that you have the money now. This is a daily practice.

CHAPTER SIX

CROSSING OVER: BE THE QUEEN

"People are like bees. They're all workers who could be queens, with the right stuff, but once a queen-making has begun, it can't be reversed."

—NATASHA PULLEY

How would it feel to have a team supporting you and doing all the things you don't want to do?

How would it feel to be surrounded by a community of women who truly have your back, lift you up, and support you to be as big and beautiful as you can possibly be?

How would it feel to know, without a shadow of a doubt, that you can be, do, and have whatever it is that you desire?

SLAVE GIRL OR QUEEN?

One of my very first coaches and the founder of Divine Living, Gina Devee, says we have a choice to be a slave girl or a Queen. It's always a choice—and you (and only you) get to make that choice for yourself, each and every single day.

As the slave girl, you give away your power. You play small, and you let your outdated beliefs and stories run your life. You don't know how to say no or yes. You are exhausted, overwhelmed, overworked, and settle for less than you deserve. You do it all yourself. You feel unsupported and are often on the verge of a breakdown. You are stuck and don't see a way out. Life happens to you and you are a victim of your circumstances. You have forgotten that you are responsible for what your life looks like. Your relationships are draining—especially your relationship with money—and there is never enough...never enough money, time, love, or energy.

As a Queen, you know how to be with the parts of yourself that need listening to. You take responsibility for your life. You know how to take your power and passion back. You make the decision and commitment to make yourself available only for what you truly desire. As a Queen you are supported, and you delegate often so that you only do what you love.

As a Queen, you are able to drop into your pleasure and exist in a relaxed, energized state of being. You serve others at a high level. You contribute and add value to the lives of others. You are highly generous and support others to the best of your ability. You feel grateful and connected. As a Queen, you know it's more about who you are being and less about what you are doing. You walk your talk. You pay attention to the way you dress and how you carry yourself. You reclaim your beauty and you own it. You know what you desire and how to bring those desires into reality. You love yourself deeply. You have a deep knowing of who you are, why you are here, and you know your soul-aligned mission and purpose. You are a willing, wise, wild woman.

So, which is it? Slave girl or Queen? It's completely up to you.

Before you choose, I want to remind you of a few things.

You can have an incredibly successful, thriving network marketing business. You can have extraordinary relationships. You can have as much money as you desire. You can have optimal health. You can have a supportive and loving community. You can have a deep and rich spiritual life. You are worthy. You are deserving. You are a Queen. You *can* have it all.

ATTRACTION MARKETING

We attract who we are. When we choose to be a Queen, we attract people like ourselves into our business. The person you choose to be—both in business and life—will determine the type of people who will show up to partner with you. You can tell what season you are truly living from by looking at the people you attract. Is your team made up of problem-focused, low energy, unmotivated, negative, stuck, glass-is-half-empty people? Or, are they driven, goal oriented, powerful, passionate, and glass-is-half-full people who can see the big vision for their lives? Are they grateful, connected, and focused on giving their gifts to others in service and contribution? Be the woman with whom you'd want to work. Be the Queen and you will start attracting people whom you are overjoyed to work with.

SISTERHOOD

A Queen is surrounded by other Queens. She has sisters in her life who support her, celebrate her, and truly have her back. And, of course, it goes without saying that she does the same for them. This sisterhood is a tremendous source of energy and inspiration.

Unfortunately, most women do not experience this level of sisterhood in their lives. There is so much competition among women. We can easily get jealous as we compare ourselves to others and feel inadequate when we see how successful, beautiful, thin, loved, or supported they are. From this place of lack, we are not able to truly be supportive and genuinely celebrate other women. Staying stuck in this lack mentality will kill your network marketing business and will further isolate you from having the support that you desire from your fellow sister affiliates. Queens do not gossip. They may sometimes feel jealous and compare themselves to others (after all, we are all human), but they know how to be with these parts by acknowledging and accepting them, and then choose something different.

You have an amazing product and opportunity and want to share it with the world. When you are in your pleasure and radiating energy, people will find their way to you. A Queen has people who flock to her, want to be around her, and want to hear what she has to share. There is more than enough for you. There is more than enough support. There is more than enough love. There are more than enough affiliates. There is more than enough money. And, there is more than enough energy.

When you're the Queen of your network marketing business, you hold the other women on your team with high regard and respect. You may want to create a culture of deep sisterhood and a place where the women on your team can come together to share their successes, get support, feel seen and heard, and have one another's backs. The women on your team lift each other up and have an opportunity to share in an experience that is so uncommon in our culture.

As I mentioned before, I conduct weekly zooms with the women on my team. One of the most rewarding things I get to experience within my business is watching the women who show up week after week to these meetings build thriving businesses in a way that feels energized, fun, and full of life force and magic.

We first do a wombspace-connecting meditation where we remember what it means to build from our .feminine pleasure and power. I then invite the women to brag about their successes. This is a practice developed by Mama Gena, who is all about empowering women to be in their pleasure. We brag not from a place of ego or conceit, but rather from a place of owning our power. When we are witnessed by other women we are changed in a profound way. It's high time that we, as women, stop playing small and instead fully own and celebrate, out loud, our wins and accomplishments, with no apology! In my opinion, women apologize way too much. Notice how many times in a day you apologize for things. Yes, if you accidentally hurt someone, apologize. But please stop apologizing for taking up space, being big, or having your voice heard. And when you receive a compliment, I want to encourage you to be bold and say, "Thank you, It's true!" That is another Mama Gena gem and it comes not from ego, but from ownership.

I would love to see more women within network marketing create a culture of sisterhood within their team. It is invaluable for women to feel supported to be as big, bold, and beautiful as they can possibly be while building a business. It is life-changing actually.

DELEGATE TO YOUR TEAM

Powerful and successful women have a team of people supporting them. Period.

As women, we get to do what we love and delegate the rest.

You don't have to do anything that you don't love to do. I know this seems like an insane statement to most of you, but it's true. Once you commit to moving from slave girl to Queen, you too will begin to see the truth in this.

Look around at your life and make a list of the things that you don't love doing. Who can you delegate those tasks to? A gardener, a house cleaner, a nanny, a personal assistant, a marketing team, or someone to help with social media? Outsource any and all tasks you don't love to do.

I also urge you to hire several professionals for your team. The first is a life coach. If you're going to really be a powerful, successful six- or seven-figure earner in the network marketing industry, you absolutely need the support of a coach—one who has gotten to the place you desire to be. You also absolutely need a good CPA and a financial advisor. Queens have teams of people helping them with their finances. I cannot emphasize this enough. If there is no container in which to manage your money, the money won't flow.

You may be saying, "That's great, but I don't have the money to hire a team. I just started my business!" I felt the very same way when one of my coaches suggested that it was time for me to find my team. This is where we will put into practice what I have shared in this book.

You create your reality, so start by making the choice and saying, "I choose to make having a team a nonnegotiable. I'm only available to be supported in this way. I have the money to pay for my team members because I have as much money as I need for all of my desires. I have an incredible team of people who do everything I don't want to do, so that I have more energy to give my gifts in service to the world."

In your morning meditation, feel the gratitude for these team members. Know who they are and how they support you. See them doing the tasks you have delegated, so that your energy can be freed up to focus on what brings you joy and lights you up.

At first, you will start with one team member. Right now, what is the one single thing that you can delegate that will provide you the greatest support? If you don't know, connect with wombspace and ask. Use your feminine pleasure and power to get what you desire. Connect with the desire, fuel it with pleasure, ignite the power, make a decision, and ask to be shown the next steps that will attract the person that can support you. And then listen for the answer.

Add this team member's pay into your money mantra as part of what you choose to make each month. Also, add this team member in the *purpose for the money* section of your mantra. Part of the purpose for the money I make each month is to pay for my incredible team that supports me. A Queen has a team around her.

You can also delegate within your organization. Some people may be really good at training. Some may be great at three-way calls. Some may be amazing at organizing events. You may want to delegate certain tasks within your organization, as long as it feels good for the people you are delegating to as well. Remember, people love the ability to give their gifts within a community. By helping people see what they are good at, and encouraging them to do more of that, everyone wins. This is where a true Queen beautifully leads her team and everyone thrives. We all work together and support each other to do what feeds us, and then we find support to help us with the areas that don't have as much energy.

GIVE GENEROUSLY

This book has helped you develop your internal team of

support. You have connected with your wombspace, temple, Healing Guide, Creating Guide, and Money Honey. You also now have a vision of the external team of support available to you within your business and life. You are cushioned by an infinite amount of unconditional support, if you choose to be. As a Queen, you know how to receive this high-level support, which allows you to give exceptional support to others through your generosity.

A Queen thinks big and knows she can have it all. Her vision is always expanding. She lives luxuriously and gives back generously. She goes on vacation, to the spa, gets massages, and spends money on clothing and jewelry that makes her feel beautiful and alive. She also gives abundantly to others and to causes that she is passionate about. She cares about the world, wants to solve problems, and contributes at a very, very high level. There is no fear of giving, because there is an endless amount of money moving through her. She lives as luxuriously as she likes and gives back in service to humanity in a hugely profound way.

SELF-CARE AND GETTING INTO ALIGNMENT

Network marketing is an unparalleled way for you to be of service and contribution, give back to others, and create a legacy for your children and grandchildren. Three to five years of focus and commitment has the potential to create a source of passive income that will hopefully last for your entire life.[6] Becoming a six- or seven-figure earner is within your grasp, but during this focused and frenzied time, you must take care of yourself and build from your pleasure and power if you want to build your business in a sustainable way.

Establish a healthy sleep pattern, exercise, meditate, and release any addictions and behaviors that are no longer serving you. Do the things that help you stay clear, focused, and energized. Take Epsom salts baths, get a massage, go to the chiropractor, or get acupuncture. Do whatever it takes to stay fueled.

Most women don't succeed because they are out of physical alignment. When you're in a state of flight or fight, your brain isn't working at full capacity and it's difficult to change habits, thought patterns, and beliefs. When you're out of alignment, you are only focused on how you can make it through the day without collapsing. Again, success in network marketing requires you to get into alignment, whether it be through chiropractic, meditation, or hemp extract (which supports your brain to achieve states similar to those of deep prolonged meditation). Commit to waking up your brain through these practices, so that you can think different thoughts, take different actions, and change your life.

---

6   Again, we never make promises or guarantees of income.

PRACTICE, PRACTICE, PRACTICE

Everything I've laid out in this book requires practice. This is a journey that will continue to unfold for the rest of your life. It takes so much more than just reading these pages once and then putting the book down. You have to make the decision, commit, and act upon it daily. So now, I ask you to make a pledge. Pledge to begin changing your life *now*. Pledge to do the actions that it takes to be wildly successful. Pledge to be the willing, wise, wild woman. Pledge to be a Queen. Email me at drerin@networkmarketingqueen.com and let me know that you made this decision. I would love to hear from you!

Here is your Queen's checklist:

- ☐ Commit to the daily practices of the willing, wise, and wild woman and practice the meditations found at the end of each chapter. All of these involve connecting to wombspace, which is the game changer for your business and life.
- ☐ State your money mantra daily with power and passion.
- ☐ Connect with your Money Honey daily.
- ☐ Gather team members to whom you can delegate all that you don't want to do.
- ☐ Exercise/self-care daily.
- ☐ Read books on empowerment and wealth consciousness for at least thirty minutes daily.
- ☐ Take pleasure breaks daily.

The more you do these practices, the more your life will change in the most magical and miraculous ways. I can promise you that.

Find an accountability partner and commit to communicating with them at least five to six days a week, even if it's a brief text letting them know what things you've accomplished. Getting yourself supported in this way will help you get from where you are to where you desire to be. Reach out to someone *now* and ask for support. Then receive it.

EXERCISE: MORNING MEDITATION

Sit in your wombspace connecting position. Close your eyes and place your hands, palm over palm, on your wombspace. Relax your shoulders and jaw and begin watching your breath. Begin to say *hello* to your wombspace by breathing slowly and deeply into your belly while allowing your pelvis to move. Find yourself being held in your temple and take inventory of any emotions that are currently present.

Is there fear? Is there discouragement? Is there hopelessness? Do you want to give up? Are you being triggered by someone on your team? Are you judging or blaming others? Are you feeling alone or unsupported? Notice what's going on without feeling the need to change anything. Become aware of, acknowledge, and just be with these feelings and parts of you.

Now, connect with your desire. Envision what your life and business are like in three months and then three years. Who are you being? What are you doing? How much money are you making? Where do you live? Where are you traveling? How many people are on your team? What is your team culture? How are you showing up as a leader in your company? How are you giving back? What kind of relationships are you engaged in? How do you feel in your body? How are you being supported? Hold these visions and desires. Sink further into your wombspace and fuel these desires with pleasure—the pleasure of your breath and movement, the pleasure of your connection to the earth, the pleasure of you being in your body, and the pleasure of how relaxed and energized you feel.

Continue breathing into and moving your pelvis and become aware of the gratitude for these desires. Be grateful for them now, even before they have manifested. Find three specific things that are already present in your business and life that you are grateful for. Focus on all of the beauty that is around you now and let this gratitude move through your whole body.

Now it's time to receive. See yourself in your temple receiving a blessing. Maybe you feel a golden light washing down over your head and through your body, making you radiant and magnetic, and connecting you to something so much bigger than yourself. Maybe you are offered a flower or other small gift. Receive this blessing fully, further opening your receiving channels to let in all of your visions and desires.

Once again, connect with the pleasure that comes from being connected to your wombspace and allow that to ignite the power. Feel yourself energized and aligned. Ask, "Whose life am I meant to bless today? What are my next soul-aligned action steps today? How can I show up more powerfully today in order for my business to thrive?" Continue connecting to wombspace through breath and movement and listen to hear the answers.

Thank your wombspace for the eternal wisdom and guidance that is always available to you here.

To receive the bonus audio meditation that accompanies this chapter, visit: networkmarketingqueen.com.

JOURNAL: DELEGATION

Write down the tasks you don't love to do and determine how and where you might begin to outsource them. Calculate the expenses so you can incorporate them into your money mantra.

....

....

....

....

....

....

....

....

....

....

CONCLUSION

THE WHOLE WOMAN:
SEASON OF INTEGRATE

Again, I want to tell you that I am sorry.

I am sorry it's been so hard for you.

I am sorry you have not been told every day that you are a beautiful, powerful, incredible woman with unique and special gifts to share with the world. I am sorry that you have not known that you can be, do, and have whatever it is that your heart and soul deeply long for.

I am sorry you haven't felt seen or heard and that you were taught that you have to settle for less than what you deserve.

I am sorry you have felt disconnected, unsupported, exhausted, and alone.

I pray that after reading these pages, you have discovered a place within you that will be an ongoing and endless well and resource of deep support and connection. I pray that you have accessed even just a little bit of your feminine power. I pray that your life has started to change and that you are opening to receiving all of the abundance that is always available to you. I pray that you are choosing to walk the path of becoming the Queen of your business and life.

You've tasted the Seasons of Discover, Awaken, and Transform. The magic now happens when you live in the Season of Integrate. You know when you are the willing woman, the wise woman, and the wild woman. The goal isn't to be in one particular season. The goal is to be aware of, acknowledge, and accept the season you are currently in—then consciously bring in more of the season that will fuel you to be the fullest expression of you.

Sometimes you just need to suffer or feel stuck, and during those times you must allow yourself to be with the emotions present. Give yourself time and space to do this, fully. Sometimes you need to pause, slow down and be more in your being and receiving, without doing a damn thing. And, sometimes you need to move forward in a fierce and powerful way and ain't nobody gonna get in your way of creating all that you desire.

When you live from this place of integration, you are the

designer of your most extraordinary life. You know how to be with challenge when it arises. You know how to get into your pleasure and how to get into your power. You know how to manifest your desires as the radiant, attractive, magnetic woman that you are. You know how to be with what is and then call in more of what you are so ready for.

And again, creating massive success by owning your feminine power is a journey—one that will bring you more joy and energy than anything else you have ever done. But, it won't always be easy.

So, if you ever feel alone, connect to wombspace, go into your temple, and remember that you've got this. You are beautiful. You are powerful. What you have to say matters. You have unique gifts to bring to the world that only you can bring. You are worthy and you deserve to have it all.

You *are* a Network Marketing Queen.

APPENDIX

RECOMMENDED READING

- *Think and Grow Rich* by Napolean Hill
- *The Science of Getting Rich* by Wallace D. Wattles
- *Feel Free to Prosper* by Marilyn Jenett
- *You are a Badass at Making Money* by Jen Sincero
- *Leveraging the Universe* by Mike Dooley
- *The Big Leap* by Gay Hendricks
- *Pussy* by Mama Gena

AUDIOS

To receive the audios that go with the meditations at the end of each chapter, go to networkmarketingqueen.com.

ACKNOWLEDGMENTS

I would first and foremost like to acknowledge my coach, friend, and sister, Christina Morassi, for the profound level of support that she gave me throughout this process. Christina, your fierce love, wisdom and ability to see me and hold space for this vision has been simply extraordinary. I am truly forever grateful for your presence in my life.

To Karin Pedersen, my tantric dance teacher—thank you for your mentorship and guidance around helping me access my center and this deep place within me. Your wisdom, support, and love over all of these years has meant more to me than you know. The way that you have truly seen me has changed me in the most profound way. There is no way this book would be in existence without you and our work together. You have helped shape me into who it is that I am today and for that I am forever grateful.

To Donny Epstein—thank you for bringing the incredible

work of NSA and ROH into the world. My work with you over the past 25 years has been one of the most important parts of my life. I wouldn't be who and where I am today without your mentorship and wisdom.

To Eileen Karpfinger—thank you for introducing me to our incredible company and to this life changing journey! I am eternally grateful for your love, support, and presence in my life as my sponsor and friend.

To Dara Ekster, mi copiloto—thank you for being my right hand woman, for being one of my greatest teachers, for challenging me, for loving me unconditionally, for helping me see myself so much more clearly and for being here for me through all of the ups and downs. I could absolutely not do what I am doing here without you by my side. I love you.

To all of the women in my network marketing company—upline, downline, and crossline. Thank you for being my greatest teachers in exploring what creating massive success by owning your feminine power looks like. Thank you for showing up so profoundly and for being so committed to this mission that we are on together. Thank you for having my back, lifting me up and for not being afraid to say the things that are hard to say in service of my growth and for being open to me doing this as well for you. This sisterhood that we are creating here is rare and special. Thank you for showing up and for being part of it.

To all of the women in my incredible Ashland community—thank you for being my greatest teachers in helping me really feel and know what true sisterhood looks and feels like. We have raised our children together, cried together, laughed together, danced together and have weathered so many storms together. Thank you for all the ways you have held me and loved me. We are so blessed to have what we do with each other and may it only get deeper and stronger. And of course, my deepest gratitude for all the men in our community as well, who celebrate us, love us, and create the container for us to be who we are and drop more fully into our relaxed feminine essence.

To Paul Rogers, John Taylor, and Austin Tice—Thank you for being my mentors and showing me the best examples of how to build as men. Thank you for seeing me, recognizing me, and bringing me in close to do what we are doing. I feel humbled and beyond honored to be working with you. I would not be where I am without your guidance and support and am forever grateful. And to all of the incredible men in our company—thank you for all that you do and for holding such strong masculine presence. It helps us women access our feminine power more than you realize.

To my best friend, Melissa. Thank you for being my biggest fan, for hashing out ideas for titles and cover images, and for just always being there and rooting me on. Your presence in my life supports me to be who I am and do what

I am doing in a huge way. Thank you for being the best assistant ever throughout the creation of this book and for lightening my load so that I could focus on this. Thank you for knowing me sometimes better than I know myself and for always knowing the perfect thing to say to help me get back on track. And thank you for always making me laugh and supporting me to not take any of it too seriously. I love you forever and always.

Thank you to my partner, Tom, for being such a strong and powerful masculine presence in my life, and for being a place that I could melt into throughout the journey of writing this book. Thank you for listening and hearing my fears, doubts, and challenges and for offering deep wisdom when I needed it. Thank you for your unconditional love and support and for deeply seeing who I am. Thank you for teaching me what it truly means to surrender into my pleasure so that I can get more into my power and give my gifts more potently to the world.

To Nikita and Cornflower—thank you for being such an integral part of my team and for all of the ways that you support me and my business. Thank you for so incredibly and lovingly holding so many of the moving parts, so that my energy can be freed up to do more of what I love. Thank you for all of your attention and presence that you've brought here in this process of writing my first book. It means the world to me and I love you both dearly.

Thank you Starla Fortunata (photographer), Sybil Henry (stylist), and Kriz Crane (make-up and hair) for being on my team and supporting me in such an extraordinary way to get this fun cover photo.

And last but not least, thank you for the team at Scribe! Nikki Katz, thank you for the incredible interviews and for holding the container for me to get all of this content out into the world. Thank you, Andrea Ho, Erin Tyler, and Cindy Curtis, for the incredible cover. Thank you, Bailey Hayes, for being an incredible publishing manager and for being such a steady support throughout this whole process. Thank you, Josh Raymer, for copywriting. Thank you, Alan Gintzler, for editing. Thank you, Ian Claudius, for the interior layout design. And thank you to Candace Sinclair for proofreading. What an incredible team you are and I am so grateful for the parts you all played in getting this message out into the world!

ABOUT THE AUTHOR

DR. ERIN POLLINGER has been a chiropractor since 1999 and is a life coach supporting people around physical and financial freedom. She owns a retreat center in Costa Rica, called Tierra Sagrada de Costa Rica, where she will be spending more time leading retreats around feminine powered leadership. She also leads workshops in the US supporting women to go deeper into the principles in this book. She is a top earner in her network marketing company and is currently traveling all over the world to support her growing team. She is also a mother of a beautiful nineteen-year-old young woman, named Willow. Dr. Erin is from New York, moved to the West Coast to go to chiropractic school when she was nineteen years old and is now based in Ashland, Oregon, where she has lived for the past nineteen years.

To learn more about Dr. Erin, go to networkmarketingqueen. com.

To find out about upcoming Costa Rica Retreats and workshops in the US, please email drerin@network marketingqueen.com.